'Ow Bist?

For all the children who attended
Little Somerford School

Crumps Barn Studio
Syde, Cheltenham GL53 9PN
www.crumpsbarnstudio.co.uk

Cover design by Lorna Gray

All photographs © the author unless otherwise specified

Typeset in Adobe Garamond Pro

All our books are printed on responsibly sourced paper from managed
woodlands and recycled material. Printed in the UK by CMP, Poole.

ISBN 978-1-915067-50-0

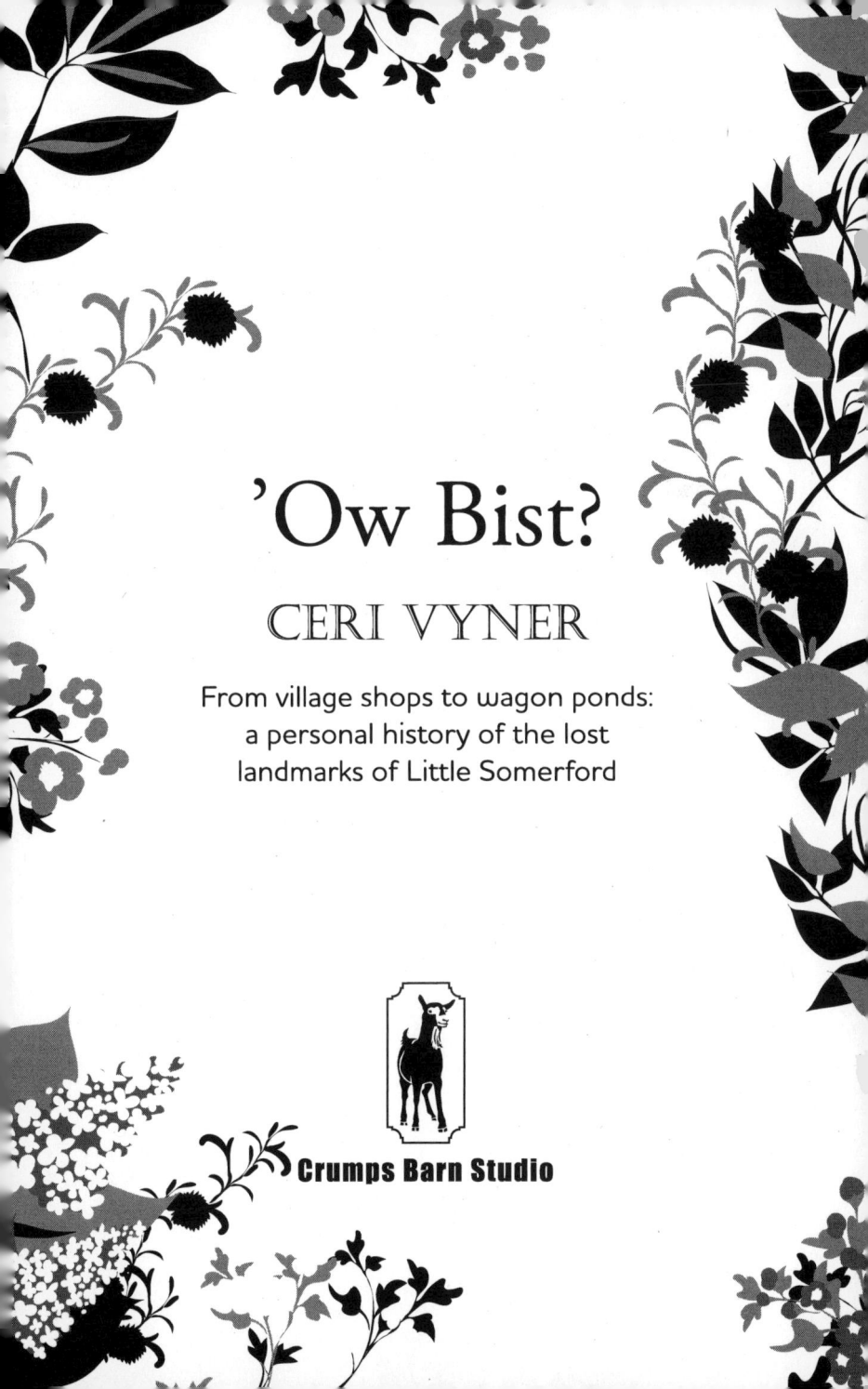

'Ow Bist?

CERI VYNER

From village shops to wagon ponds:
a personal history of the lost
landmarks of Little Somerford

Crumps Barn Studio

LANDMARKS AND HISTORIES OF LITTLE SOMERFORD

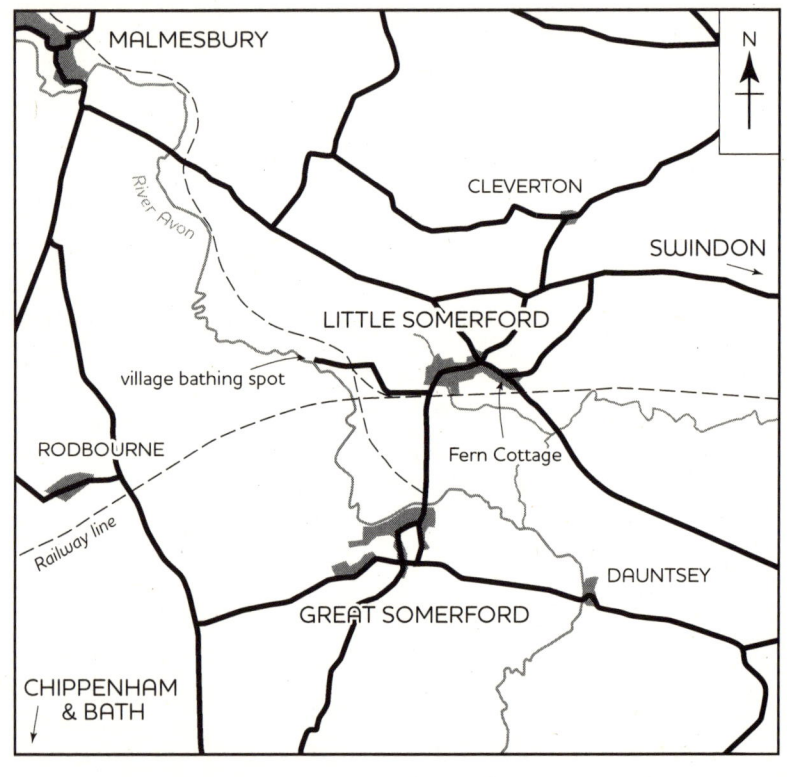

Map of Little Somerford and nearby towns c.1950
(not to scale)

INTRODUCTION

WILTSHIRE is an inland county in South West England, bordered on all sides by the counties of Gloucestershire, Oxfordshire, Berkshire, Hampshire, Dorset and Somerset. Its countryside includes rolling chalk downlands, and Salisbury Plain in the south of the county. The northern part is characterised by attractive villages built of the local creamy-gold limestone. The houses blend beautifully into the surrounding countryside and over many years develop a soft, luminous colour as if the sunlight has soaked into the stones.

Little Somerford in the 1950s and 60s was an exceptionally pretty village in North Wiltshire. Situated on the southern edge of the Cotswolds, it lies in a fertile valley between the River Avon on one side and Brinkworth Brook, a tributary of the Avon, on the other. It is a nucleated village set in undulating countryside and green meadows. Small mixed farms with cattle, a few pigs or sheep, and poultry meant that the old meadows were seldom ploughed then and contained many varieties of wildflowers. The smell of sweet meadow hay scented the whole village at harvest time. In some fields the old ridge and furrow could clearly be seen.

My family moved to Little Somerford in February 1954 when I was just fourteen months old.

We lived in a largely unmodernised cottage, the kind

that would be condemned today. It had electricity, but no indoor bathroom or toilet and just one cold water tap and none of the household items which most people would consider essential these days. Nevertheless, it had the most lovely cottage garden which we depended on for fruit and vegetables, and its beauty made a lasting impression on me.

Little Somerford then was a real community which revolved around the village school, the church of St John the Baptist, the garage, shop, public houses and the village hall. People knew their neighbours and helped them where necessary.

Everyone in Little Somerford greeted each other if they met one or more of their neighbours. Not to do so was considered un-neighbourly or 'to have airs above your station!'

The usual greeting amongst the men was a finger lifted to the brim of their cap or up to their temple, accompanied by 'Ow bist?' (How are you?) The village women sometimes said 'Ow bist?' but more often just 'Hello.'

During the late nineteen-sixties, as new houses were built and the community grew larger, the traditional 'Ow bist?' greeting was confined to a few of the older villagers. We were taught from infancy to say hello to everyone we met in the village and to stop and speak to them and answer politely if they spoke to us. As a result of this everyone spoke to me and some of the more elderly villagers, as I grew older, told me stories of their own childhood or what had happened at the village school in *their* day, so that I was the lucky recipient of a number of interesting facts about the village.

Village people who have grown up there are fond of Little Somerford. I remember once when I was twelve, my mother and I were in the garden when a car stopped near our gate. In the car was an old lady of ninety-four and her two daughters. The old lady had been born in the village, in a cottage up East End Lane, but had moved away when she was eight. However, she never forgot the village and her daughters told us that she had talked about it constantly when they were growing up. For her birthday, their mother had requested a trip back to Little Somerford and her daughters had told her that it would all have changed, that her memories would be spoilt. The wonderful thing was that at that time the village had hardly changed at all. The housing estate had not yet been built, the village school and shop were still open. The old lady was delighted and we were pleased for her that her childhood home was as she remembered.

More recently, after sending several emails attaching information about the village to a friend who had left the village in his early teens, I sent an apology fearing I had sent too much. I was delighted to receive a reply saying: 'Anything you can ever send me about Little Somerford will make my day.'

This book has new information which was not included in my first volume *Let'n Went*.

I have tried to write down as many of my own memories about Little Somerford as I can, along with recollections shared by the people I knew back then.

Village life and the landmarks which mattered to us have changed so much. They are a part of history – the experience of young children today growing up in the village is vastly different from our experiences, which although not so very long ago, seem like a different world – so I want to record them before they are lost.

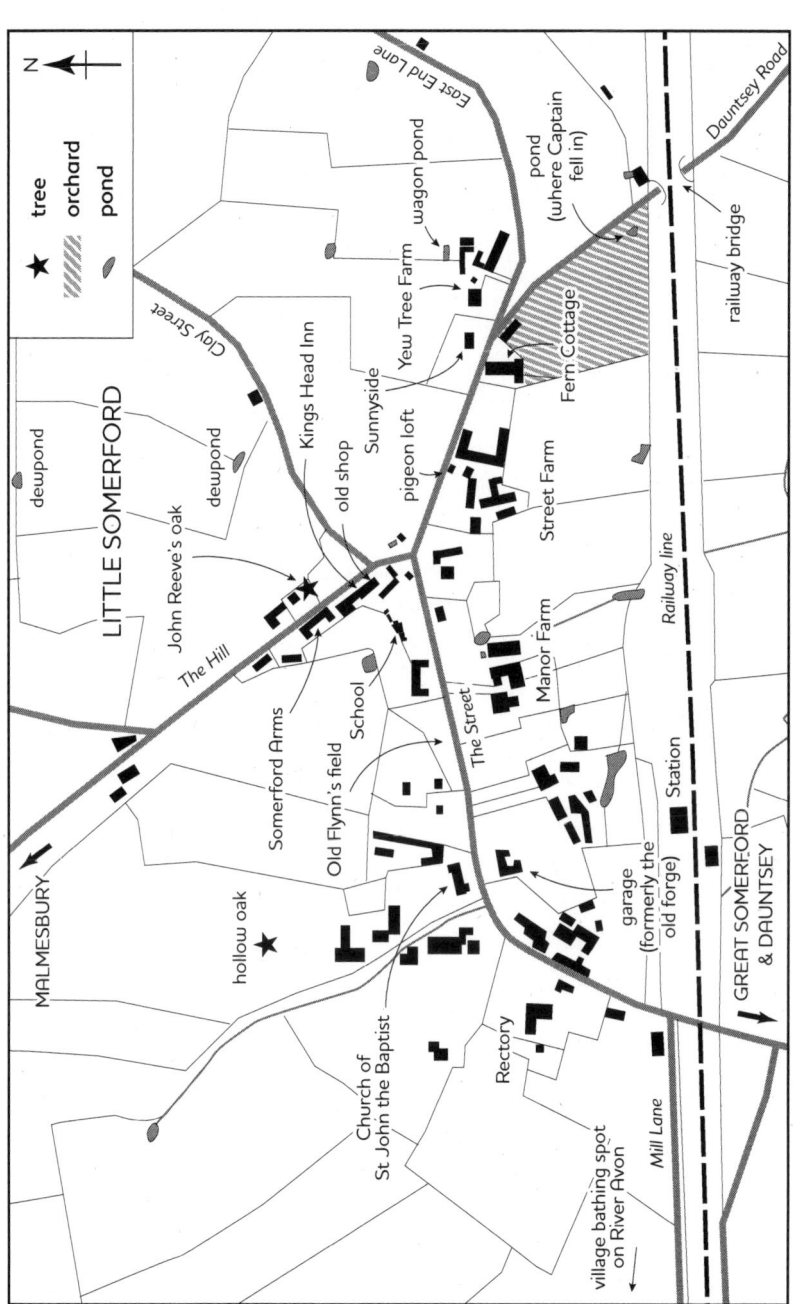

Map of Little Somerford, showing location of ponds and landmarks (not to scale)

*The former Kings Head pub. The old shop was
in the room on the right of the door*

CHAPTER 1

THE OLD SHOP

DURING THE EARLY 1950s when we first moved to Little Somerford, the village shop was in part of the building which was The Kings Head public house. This was just past Little Somerford corner. There was a short stretch of pavement outside and it was also where the Chippenham to Malmesbury bus stopped every two hours on its way through the village. The Three Crowns public house, now the Somerford Arms, was a little further along on the same side of the road.

The Kings Head at that time was run by Mr and Mrs House. The front door was in the centre of the building and when you faced the door, the tap room was on the left hand side and the right hand side was the shop. The shop counter was presided over by a lady called Mrs Huntley who worked in the shop and served customers.

Previously, the pub and shop had been run by a woman called Fanny Preddy and her name and the painted statement that she was licensed to sell beer, spirits and tobacco was still faintly seen above the front door when we were children (1950s) as it became exposed when the public house closed and Mr House's enamel nameplate was removed.

The shop in those days was an amazing place to a

small child. Whenever I entered, I would step down into this dimly lit room and it always took a minute or two for my eyes to adjust after the light outside. The next thing I always noticed was a positive barrage of aromas. This comprised a mixture of cheese, cured bacon and tea, together with an underlying earthy smell from the sacks of potatoes and carrots stored in soil on the floor at the side of the counter. Bacon was not sold in plastic packets as it is today, but was sliced off a side of bacon which was stored hung from a large hook in a beam above the counter and probably tasted all the better from absorbing all the shop aromas. The side of bacon was lifted down when it was needed and slices carved off it. Sugar was sold both loose and as lump sugar. The lump sugar was slightly cheaper because we had to break it up ourselves and it came in long rectangular 'loaves' which were wrapped in paper.

I remember being with my mother in the shop when she bought a loaf of sugar and later helping to break it up so that some of it could be used to make a cake. The loose sugar was not in packets on a shelf as it is today, but was weighed loose and poured into a sugar-paper bag folded up by the shop keeper. This sugar paper was either a dark blue or purple colour. We did not buy the more expensive loose sugar very often so we used to ask our neighbour, Kate Reeve if she had any sugar paper to spare for drawing. This type of paper is no longer used for sugar bags, but it is often used in schools for artwork paper and it is still called sugar paper after its original use.

I remember my mother allowing me to ask for something for the first time. I must have been about four years old at the time. 'I don't know your name!' I stated.

'It's Mrs Huntley', came the reply. So I had to frame my request, 'Please, Mrs Huntley, please may I have some loaf sugar.'

'Good girl,' came the reply, 'yes, of course you can.'

Mrs Huntley was a tall lady with grey shoulder length hair at that time. She was very pleasant and patient with small children taking time to decide which sweets to choose. Sometimes mixing two kinds of loose sweets, which were stored in jars, even when I only had thruppence to spend.

The counter itself was very high with a huge old-fashioned decorative till on one end of it. As a small child I could not see the countertop very clearly because it was above my head and so I had to stand back from it to get a proper look or to talk to Mrs Huntley if I was allowed to ask for something. The top of the counter was a marble slab so that it could be wiped down easily. Cheese was cut from a big block with the aid of a cheese wire, a length of sharp wire with two special ends for the shop keeper to hold so that the wire did not cut their fingers. The cheese was a type of Cheddar and came in two strengths: Medium or Strong.

On a shelf behind the counter was a long row of large, round tin cannisters with numbers on. The tins were a deep apple green in colour and the numbers were gold coloured and glowed in the dim light of the shop. The cannisters contained loose tea and coffee, and other dry goods, although we often drank Brooke Bond tea, which came in small green paper packets, and between the inner and outer wrapping was a small collectable card. These tea cards were part of a set and depicted such things as British Wild Flowers, British Wild Life, Freshwater Fishes, African Wild Life, British Butterflies and so on, with a picture on the front and information on the back. I always felt these were very educational, but they were also a wonderful way of promoting the product because parents would continue to buy the tea if their child was collecting the cards. These tea cards were very similar to cigarette cards which were being phased out at that time, but which came with certain brands of cigarettes. My brothers and I would stick our cards in albums and swap the rest with the other children at school. All tea was loose leaf tea then, there were no teabags.

Mrs Huntley always served the customers – we had to request the groceries we needed. People did not help themselves or fill a basket as they do today. She sold all the essentials, such as Lifebuoy soap in long yellow bars about ten inches long and my mother would hack pieces off when she wanted it for washing laundry or scrubbing floors. There were boxes of washing powder such as Daz and Persil. There was also an item called a Blue Bag which was put in a copper or twin tub washing machine with white clothes when they were washed and it helped to whiten them. Although my mother washed clothes by hand because we did not have a washing machine, she still used a Blue Bag in the final rinse because the yellow Lifebuoy soap made at that time made the clothes slightly yellow.

The Blue Bag had other uses too. Once when we were visiting Yew Tree Farm, my brother, B gave a yell and clutched his arm. He had been stung by a bee.

'Quick,' said Kate Reeve, 'get the sting out and then rub it with this Blue Bag, It will stop the pain.'

'I never knew that!' remarked my mother, quickly applying the blue bag to the sting.

'Yes,' replied Kate, 'There's something in it which works on stings.'

Bristows shampoo could be bought in individual sachets and there was not the wide choice of hair products there is today. One sachet of shampoo was used for my hair and my mother's hair. We rarely went to the hairdresser, and then only for a haircut. Although during the 1960s, my mother had several perms which were very fashionable then.

Some biscuits were sold loose at that time, by weight, but we usually had a mixture of broken biscuits which were sold more cheaply. If we were lucky there were often deliciously crumbly Digestive biscuits or sugar-coated sponge fingers in the mix.

When I was about five years old, the Kings Head public house closed and the shop was moved to part of the Three Crowns public house just up the road although this time it had a separate entrance from the pub. The Three Crowns was run by Mr Bert and Mrs Joyce Carroll, but Mrs Huntley was still in charge of the shop, although Mrs Carroll would sometimes serve shop customers too. If you asked Mrs Carroll about the taste or quality of any item you always received the same reply:

'Our Bert 'ad it fer 'is supper larst night and 'e said it was delicious!'

The new shop counter was lower and goods were arranged on shelves. There was a greater variety of sweets and other foodstuffs in stock, but it did not have the atmosphere of the old shop as more goods were sold in packets by then. Loaf sugar went out of fashion and all loose sugar came ready packed in bags. Convenience foods soon became commonplace and shops such as the one in our village installed refrigerators so that they could stock such delicacies as ice cream, frozen peas and Fish Fingers.

CHAPTER 2

THE RAILWAY

THE GREAT WESTERN Railway line ran along the southernmost edge of our village in a protective curve. It was built on a substantial grassed embankment which carried the line across the fields onto a brick viaduct of thirteen arches which enabled the trains to cross the River Avon and the marshy water meadows on either side. This was the main line from Swindon to Cardiff.

It was built by a team of navvies in 1903. Mr Alfred Reeve, who farmed at Street Farm at that time, was paid a substantial amount for the railway running over his land. There were brick tunnels at intervals along the embankment so that cows could get to the further fields beyond the line. A lot of material must have been brought in to build such a substantial structure.

The railway embankment soon became an important feature for attracting wildlife. Rabbits lived happily on its lower slopes, their burrows hidden by clumps of brambles. Wildflowers grew in its shelter and walking along a footpath on the far side of the embankment, I was astonished to see a variety of blue butterflies which we never saw in our garden, just a field away. These were Common Blues and Small Blue butterflies. Obviously, there must have been different plants here which provided the right food for them and the embankment protected them from the weather. I suppose to a butterfly, a railway embankment composed of chalky soil, is not dissimilar to a chalk downland.

The railway was a background to our lives and it was always clearly visible as the embankment had to be kept clear of vegetation because of the fire risk from the sparks from the steam engines' boilers. On more than one occasion there was a fire on the embankment which was not only a danger to the railway, but to fields of crops beside the line. I know that the Reeves who farmed at Yew Tree Farm were careful not to allow vegetation at the bottom of their orchard to get too near the line and a couple of times a year a team of men were seen clearing away brambles and undergrowth along the embankment.

When I was a small child we used to see and hear the huge Great Western steam engines hurtling along the track, pulling long lines of coaches or loaded wagons and giving a loud blast on their whistles as they approached Little Somerford Station. Sometimes they stopped near the railway bridge on the Dauntsey Road to take on water from the tank beside the line. My brothers and I, when we were small, often stood under the railway bridge on the Dauntsey Road when the train thundered overhead – the bridge juddered and trembled at its onslaught and smoke and steam enveloped us in a grey cloud. The noise was amplified by the bridge so I always found it a fearful experience, not being over-fond of deafening engine noises, but my brothers loved it so I had to endure it too.

We often noticed that the trains sounded louder when it was about to rain and rushed into the garden to move half-dry washing under cover before the approaching rainstorm.

Back in those days of steam, small schoolboys often declared their ambition of being an engine driver when they grew up, such was their admiration for steam trains, just as today children want to be a sports star or be on television. One classmate of ours at primary school, Malcolm Stoneham, gained great kudos for having a father who was an engine driver. Mr Ken Stoneham often drove the express trains on our main line from Swindon to Cardiff and back and could be regularly seen in mid-afternoon, returning from his early shift in his blue overalls and peaked cap. On one occasion we had an infant class outing where we walked down to the Dauntsey Road railway bridge, only about a ten minute walk from our classroom. There we all lined up to wave to Mr Stoneham as he drove the passenger train. By prior arrangement there were several shrill blasts on the whistle as the train approached and it slowed down, enabling Ken Stoneham to wave to us all from his cab. We all waved back with great enthusiasm, pointing with admiration at the huge engine as it passed through, before we excitedly walked back to school to write about our experience and draw pictures of trains.

After a few years the steam trains went out of service with the advent of diesel engines and then in their turn were replaced by electric trains which were much quieter.

There was no longer a need to clear all the bushes and trees on the embankment except where they overhung the line and so the modern trains can hardly be seen or heard, meaning that their impact is considerably reduced. The magic of the steam train has gone and little boys no longer aspire to be engine drivers.

CHAPTER 3

PONDS

CAPTAIN TAKES A PADDLE

THERE WERE a number of ponds around the village. Some were clay pits, dug out when the clay was needed; perhaps taken away to make bricks or used in the building of the railway embankment. One such was the pond at the far end of the Reeves' orchard which was opposite Yew Tree Farm and right next to our garden at Fern Cottage. We were warned never to try to paddle in this pond as it was a clay pit and likely to have steep sides and sticky clay at the bottom, both of these things would create serious problems for any child who fell in, and not only a child!

One very dark evening when gusts of wind and spats of rain pounded against our windowpanes and the sashes rattled in their frames, there was a loud knock at the door. My father got up to answer it and we all peered through the half-closed living room door to see who was out on such a dreadful evening. Charles Reeve stood there in the pouring rain, his cap pulled low over his forehead and an old hessian sack slung around his shoulders to keep the worst of the rain from soaking his jacket.

'The horse has got himself in the pond and can't get

out. We've got the fire brigade. Can you come and help pull him out?' Charles asked.

'Of course, I'll come straight away, I'll just get my coat,' replied my father, and after a few more brief words Charles hurried away. Our father grabbed his coat and put his head round the living room door to inform my mother what was happening. Captain, the Reeves' carthorse had stumbled into the pond in the dark and his hooves had stuck in the wet clay at the bottom. Without human help he would drown.

We were all very worried for Captain as we all liked him and hated the thought of him coming to harm.

B begged to go and watch and M and I looked up hopefully. Our parents quickly decided that B could go, but not M or me. Our mother fussed around B making sure his coat was buttoned up, his wellingtons on and his head protected by a woollen balaclava helmet. He was given the spare torch to hold and reminded not to get in the way of the important rescue operation.

I remember my father describing the horse's rescue later that evening. My father and B rushed off, up the path to the road then round the corner to the orchard gate. They could see the lights of the fire engine illuminating the scene at the far end of the field and men moving about. Two men were in the water. One of the Reeve brothers stood up to his chest in the pond, trying to calm the frightened horse. A young fireman was trying to swim under Captain with a sling by which he could then be hauled out. The men in the water had ropes around their waists in case they lost their footing and to enable them to be freed if they too became stuck in the clay.

B watched in great excitement as the young fireman managed to swim under the horse and secure the sling. Then came the difficult task of freeing Captain's hooves one at a time, without him panicking and kicking his rescuers in his fear. The fireman had to be helped out of the pond and John Reeve in the water had to keep clear as Captain lurched around trying to get his footing, but also be ready to assist when Captain's hooves became stuck again, which they did. After several attempts and with a great deal of splashing, whinnying and snorting on the part of Captain, as the sides of the pond were steep, the team of men on the bank managed to pull him out and he stood wet, muddy and frightened on the field.

After a quick check over by a vet, as far as it could be done by torchlight and in pouring rain, to make sure Captain had not sustained any serious injury, he was covered with a horse rug and led away to his stable. William and John Reeve were experts in the care of heavy horses, having looked after them since they were boys. They were going to give Captain a good rub down and a hot bran mash to help him recover from his dreadful ordeal. They would also check up on him throughout the night in case he needed further help. Then, warm and dry and rugged-up in his warm stable, with a full hay net and water bucket. Captain could get some well-earned rest.

*Dewponds
(image by Ceri Vyner,
with kind permission
of Hector Cole)*

THE DEWPONDS

THERE WAS a dewpond at the top of Little Nurnalls, a field which was once part of what had once been Somerford Down, at least it is labelled such on old maps of Wiltshire. Somerford Down was a chalk ridge sheltering the village in the valley below. Eventually it was enclosed and hedges divided the area into fields.

Dew ponds are manmade saucer-shaped ponds dug into chalk and lined with clay to enable it to hold rainwater. They were essential sources of water for grazing sheep or cattle until modern farming enabled farmers to install water troughs connected to a mains supply.

This pond was one of several just below the ridge. It was there for almost all the year although it dried up in hot summers, but it supported a surprising amount of wildlife. It was quite shallow, perhaps a foot deep in the centre and less at the sloping edges and about seven feet across when I knew it, but it was almost certainly larger and deeper originally as they silt up if they are not maintained, but once mains water had been installed nearby, and a cattle trough connected to it, there was not so much need for the pond.

There was sometimes a small amount of frogspawn in the dewpond, but not often, which makes me wonder whether the frogs knew that a wet spring and early summer would enable their offspring to survive. Pond skaters skittered across the surface and small water creatures existed in the inch or two of wet clay at the bottom. It was overhung at one side by a pussy willow tree and I had permission to cut a few of the smaller branches in spring as I loved the furry softness of the catkins.

The pond provided water for a variety of wild animals, including the hares which nestled in their form lower down the slope, the fox which slunk along the hedge and the slow worms which basked in the sunshine on the drier soil further along the field.

There was a second dewpond in Little Nurnalls, but this one was at the bottom corner of the field which sloped down to it. This pond dried up more quickly than the one higher up, but oxlips, cowslips and buttercups loved the extra moisture in this sheltered dip. Another pussy willow tree grew near it in the hedge. The wonderful thing about this field was that it had never been ploughed and I was astonished to notice one day that some of the buttercups had mutated so much that they had as many as twelve or fourteen petals compared to the usual five on most buttercups. I always came to this field in Spring to see and smell the cowslips and to admire the oxlips, both of which were becoming a rarity when I was a child. Further up the field delicate white violets grew in the shelter of the hawthorn hedge which was a mass of blossom in May.

I was delighted to see recently that one of these dewponds still exists continuing to provide an important habitat for the local wildlife.

B AND THE LEECH

ONCE, WHEN I was about five, we had an encounter with a leech. My older brothers went for a walk and went to investigate a pond. I think this was the wagon pond which had a firm surface on the bottom of it as otherwise B would not have gone for a paddle. After about half an hour, M rushed into our house:

'Come and help B, quick! There's a worm on his leg and he can't get it off. It's biting him. We tried to pull it off, but it won't let go!'

'Where is he?' enquired my mother. 'Ceri, go and get your father.' I ran to my father's study and asked him to come and help and we all rushed to the front door.

B came limping down the path, stopping to look with horror at what looked like a small, black worm attached to his left calf.

'Oh, it's a leech!' exclaimed our father. 'You won't be able to pull it off, you'll have to wait until it drops off.'

'Get it off! Get it off!' shouted B.

'It won't hurt you. It'll drop off in a minute, just stand still,' said our father putting a hand on B's shoulder to calm him. 'I haven't seen a leech for years!' he added in an interested tone, 'not since I was a boy.'

We watched in fascination as the tiny black worm-like creature writhed and stretched on B's leg. Suddenly it grew much fatter.

'Ah, it's sucking the blood out now,' said our father in satisfaction. 'It'll drop off in a minute.'

'Ugh, it's horrible!' protested B.

'People used to pay to have leech treatments,' said our father, trying to convince B that the leech was not as bad as he thought.

The leech quadrupled in size so that it was about four inches long and as wide as a large fat earthworm, then it detached itself and dropped onto the path.

Blood trickled down B's calf and our mother declared her intention of applying Savlon to the wound. Our father reluctantly disposed of the leech, saying that they were probably a rarity now and reminding B and M not to paddle in that particular pond in future.

THE WAGON POND

NEAR THE BACK gateway to Yew Tree farmyard at the side of Long Ground was the wagon pond. This wagon pond was made for a specific purpose as can be seen by its rectangular shape on the OS maps of the village. It was about eighteen inches deep in the centre and shallower at the edges as it sloped gently down to the middle. It had a firm floor of cobbles so that wagons could be driven in and out safely without the horse becoming stuck in mud. Wagon ponds were very important because in the days of horse-drawn wagons, it was essential to regularly soak the cart wheels in hot weather so that the felloes – the wooden rim to which the spokes are fixed – swelled and gripped the iron tyre firmly. If the wheel were to dry out, the wood would shrink back from the metal tyre and would be in danger of falling apart.

John Constable's picture of *The Hay Wain* shows a wagon pond with a horse and cart in it. The horse is not just having a drink, the wagon wheels are getting a soaking.

This one was used by the Reeves until 1958 when Captain, their last carthorse was sold. It was convenient to have the wagon pond by the back gate of the farmyard because the horse and wagon could be driven through it at the end of a hot day's work or at the start of the working day. Being near the farm gate it would also serve as a reminder to a busy farmer to preserve his wagon wheels.

Unfortunately, the wagon pond is no longer essential and it has been filled in.

CHAPTER 4

SWIMMING NEAR KINGSMEAD MILL

IN VERY HOT WEATHER we always pleaded with our mother to come with us down to the River Avon not far from Kingsmead Mill, where there was a spot where many villagers gathered to enjoy a paddle or a swim. We were not allowed down on our own, because part of the river there was very deep, but if we had friends who were going we were allowed to join them.

Three quarters of the way down Mill Lane, within sight of the mill, there was a field gate on the left hand side of the road. We would climb the gate and walk diagonally across the field to the River Avon and cross it by a bridge. The river meandered under this bridge towards the viaduct at the far left hand edge of the field, which carried the railway line across the river and water meadow. Sometimes we wandered down to admire the viaduct and marvel at its engineering. One of the older villagers told me that as a boy, they had often gone down to watch the viaduct being built.

Not far from the viaduct we could see the old Second World War pill box with its grassy top which we sometimes climbed. At the bridge we would pause to admire the river, the patches of green water weed growing in the gravelly bottom and the freshwater fish darting about. However, we usually turned right after crossing the bridge and cut across the field in the other direction towards the Mill, where the river curved round in several meanders creating a gravelly, sheltered beach. This was where the villagers met together as the water was shallow enough for small children to paddle and cool themselves down. Further along the water was deeper and adults could have a swim. I remember one tall youth wading along the river there. The water was just above his knees when suddenly he sank up to his neck as he encountered a deep bore hole which he said was full of fish. Luckily, he was a good swimmer, but it showed that one had to swim with caution down there.

The water was extremely cold because several springs came down through the chalk and flowed out into the river. My parents allowed me to drink the pure, cold spring water, but never the water from the river which might have fertiliser residue from the field. Bill Archard and his family who lived in the Level Crossing cottage not far away, did not have a water supply in their cottage and obtained it from another spring a bit further up, nearer their cottage. I know this to be so because Bill Archard told us. He had to fetch his family's drinking water twice a day, which was all very well in summer, but not so pleasant on a freezing winter morning.

A number of families would take picnics and flasks of tea and bottles of fruit squash for their children and many a hot summer afternoon was spent sitting in the sun on the shingle, watching the river and the children paddling or wading in the water to cool down. There was the chatter of the adults, the shrieks and laughter of children splashing each other with cold water and the gentle flow of the river. After our paddle or swim we would run out, picking our way between sharp stones to find a place to sit in the sunshine on our damp towels and warm our now frozen bodies and listen to the conversations going on around us. By the late afternoon there was often a cold breeze along the river, so two o'clock until four was the optimum time to enjoy it. Then it was time to go home and at about half past four, families began to gather their belongings and head back home. Some had left their car at the field gate, but I always enjoyed the walk back, pausing at the gate to admire beautiful Kingsmead Mill, its soft, pale gold stone reflecting back the evening sunshine before I turned back up the lane towards the centre of the village.

There were footpaths along the river and behind Kingsmead Mill and beyond that was Angrove Wood, which was turned into a nature reserve. We walked along a footpath by the river one day with our mother. The Avon there was very deep and still and when our mother later told John Reeve about our walk and asked him about the mill, he warned her not to let us too near the river there. The water apparently undercuts the bank in places and is very dangerous because the river is very deep in that stretch. John Reeve told us that when he was a boy (1890s) a horse and cart fell in the river there because the farmer did not realise that the bank was undercut and he drove the cart too near the edge. The bank gave way and the cart tipped into the river, dragging the poor horse in too. The farmer just managed to jump clear, but was devastated at the loss of his poor horse. We kept away from there after hearing that.

There is now no public right of way in that part of Mill Lane and so access to the field and the village gathering place is closed.

CHAPTER 5

DOLLY AND THE VICAR'S LIFT

AFTER OUR much loved rector Mr Lutley retired, our village had a series of temporary clergy. They were supported by the wonderful village ladies who planned and organised the Church Fete and Christmas Bazaar, and arranged the church flowers. One such lady was our kindly neighbour Mrs Dolly Iles.

The name Dolly is normally short for Dorothy, but Mrs Iles's name was Caroline. She told me that when she was tiny, her father said that she looked just like a doll, with her beautiful big blue eyes in a round face. Thereafter, everyone called her Dolly.

Dolly used to arrange the church flowers and quite often came round to ask for some greenery from our abundant garden. She did not like to ask for flowers too often, so one time when we had plenty of flowers out, my mother sent me over to Dolly's house with a message:

'Mum says we have lots of lovely flowers out at the moment, so come and pick some if you need them for the church.'

'Thank you, but I don't know as I'll be doin' the

church flowers any more,' she said sadly.

'Oh!' I replied, surprised. Dolly had always loved doing the church flower arrangements.

'Well,' continued Dolly, 'I went up The Hill last Tuesday to catch the bus into Malmesbury to do my shopping as usual, and the vicar came by in his car and stopped to give me a lift. At first, I was pleased. It had saved me the bus fare, but when we got to the Cross Hayes in Malmesbury, he said *That'll be one and sixpence, please!*'

'What!' I exclaimed.

'Well, I was so surprised you could have knocked me down with a feather, but that's what he said, and I was so shocked I paid up,' stated Dolly miserably.

'But if he was going into Malmesbury anyway …?'

'He was, he said he had a meeting.'

I was horrified. 'We sometimes get given lifts, but nobody charges if they are going into Malmesbury themselves. It would be different if we asked somebody for a lift in an emergency. We would expect to pay then.'

'That's right,' said Dolly, 'and he even charged me more than the bus fare, and he *knows* I always do the church flowers because I told him!'

Dolly was clearly very upset, and I was upset on her behalf, thinking of all the things she did for others in the village, with no thought of remuneration. I did not know what to say to comfort her, so I just said goodbye and rushed home to tell my family.

My parents were appalled too. 'Just don't accept a lift from the vicar,' I stated.

'I'll know what to say to *him!*' stated my father grimly.

The following week, my father returned from town and told us that he had been given a lift into Malmesbury by the vicar.

'How much did he charge?' asked my mother, laughing.

'Nothing!'

'What, *nothing?* How did you manage that?'

'Well, I knew I didn't have much time, so the minute I got in his car, I said, 'Do you know, Vicar, I've heard that some people in the village actually charge their neighbours for a lift into Malmesbury when they are going there anyway! Don't you think that's an un-Christian thing to do?'

"Yes," he said. And by that time we were already in Malmesbury so I jumped out of the car as soon as he stopped, and he didn't dare charge me.'

That was the last we heard of that vicar charging for lifts into Malmesbury, and villagers with cars continued to offer free lifts to their neighbours if they saw them at the bus stop, just as they always had done. We were a community.

Fern Cottage front garden c.1970

Fern Cottage kitchen garden c.1970s

CHAPTER 6

SUNDAYS

SUNDAYS WERE VERY different in the 1950s and 1960s. Firstly, nearly all shops were closed except for grocery shops and Newsagents which were open for part of the day. Our village shop opened in the morning. My brother M – he was two years older than me, while B was four years older – cycled to Malmesbury every Sunday to get a paper. The newsagent there closed at eleven o'clock in the morning,

Our village was almost silent on Sundays. We were expected to play quietly in the garden and not run around too much or make much noise. On Sundays we were not allowed to go roaming over the fields to make camps or play on a neighbouring farm as we usually did on other days when we were not at school. We also had to help with household jobs on Sunday mornings. I was always expected to polish the brass door furniture (doorknobs, letterbox, bell pull) or help with furniture polishing indoors. In summer, I picked soft fruit so that my mother could make a pie or crumble for our pudding. Most people had a proper Sunday lunch which meant a roast meal, usually beef, pork or lamb. Chicken was for special occasions then. With the meat we had vegetables from the garden. Other Sunday morning jobs included finishing school homework, and ironing and hanging up school clothes and polishing shoes ready for the school week. The rabbit and guinea pig had to be fed and watered as usual and their hutches had to be cleaned out.

There was a church service in the village church of St John the Baptist which was attended by many of the villagers. We would hear the church bells ringing and see our neighbours hurrying down the road. Kate Reeve told me that the church bells said:

'Hang Tom Fry for Telling a Lie'

John Reeve left money in his Will so that the church bells could be rung electronically. We did not go to church unless it was a special occasion such as Harvest Festival, but I did attend Sunday School in the afternoon. There I met up with several school friends and we listened to a Bible Story and discussed it and sometimes we drew pictures to illustrate the story. At the end of the session we were given a coloured picture like a Biblical postage stamp to stick in a notebook and our attendance was recorded. Sometimes the vicar dropped in to talk to us. The Sunday School was run by Mrs Iris Gleed, one of our near neighbours and I knew her well as we used to buy our eggs from her.

Even the local farmers tried to have a bit of a rest on Sundays, although animals always had to be fed and mucked out, cows had to be milked and in summer, of course, the important job of harvesting went on regardless of the day if the weather was fine. We would hear the steady hum of the milking machine or the sound of the bailer as the cut hay was turned into bales, but otherwise a strange quietness descended on the village and if I was outside I would listen to the silence. I could even hear the contented clucking of John Reeve's hens as they searched for insects in their pen behind Sunnyside.

Some village men would dig their gardens or work on their allotments on Sunday mornings, while their wives cooked their lunch. Allotments were very important for any villagers who did not have much garden. Nearly everybody grew vegetables and these were also a very competitive section in the produce classes at the Somerford Show. Women were expected to do the housework and cooking then as fewer women went out to work or if they did go out to work, many of them worked part-time. Any local cafes in little towns such as Malmesbury would be closed on Sundays. People did not go out for lunch or brunch as they might do today. Public houses did not serve food except for the occasional pickled egg from a jar on the counter or bag of peanuts or crisps from a box behind the bar. Sometimes couples would go to the village pub for a drink before Sunday lunch, but usually this was a special occasion not a regular happening.

If a particular day such as Bonfire Night happened to fall on a Sunday, then any fireworks were always held on the previous Friday or Saturday. Nobody would consider holding such a celebration on a Sunday.

Usually after a big Sunday lunch, many villagers would take a walk. We would be listening to *Gardener's*

Question Time on the radio which my mother depended on for gardening advice, before we cleared the lunch table and started washing up. If we looked out of the window we would see several neighbours walking past on their afternoon walk obviously heading up East End Lane. Sometimes we walked down to Kingsmead Mill which was a pretty walk in spring when the roadside verges were scattered with primroses and celandines.

In the late afternoon, I often accompanied my mother over to Yew Tree Farm to chat to Kate Reeve. Over a cup of tea, my mother would impart the village news. Sometimes Kate would add extra information which she had heard herself, but usually we kept her up to date on village events and news. My mother and Kate would discuss matters while I listened with interest. Then my mother would say: 'Don't you say anything about *that* or there'll be trouble!' and I would smile and agree. One had to be very careful and often diplomatic about passing news on.

On Sunday evenings we often listened to a play on the radio such as: *Play for Today* Sometimes we played cards or *Monopoly* or read a book. Then after my brothers and I had reluctantly retreated to our beds to read for half an hour, I would lie awake and listen to the faint strains of *Sing Something Simple* which my parents listened to downstairs. This was a radio programme which played popular classical music. There was also: *Your Hundred Best Tunes* which was a similar programme aimed at calming down adults after a hard week.

Most people in the village had a television and

sometimes, if there was a very good serial on television when I was a teenager, such as Galsworthy's *The Forsyte Saga* or Anthony Trollope's *Barchester Towers*, my mother and I were occasionally invited to Yew Tree Farm to watch them with Kate Reeve as we had no television at Fern Cottage.

The school, with kitchen on right
(image kindly supplied by Arlene Bishop)

CHAPTER 7

SCHOOL SPORTS DAY

OUR VILLAGE SCHOOL sports day was held near the end of the summer term when the weather was likely to be fine. It would also help to calm the high spirits of children already anticipating a long summer holiday free of school. The school playground was tiny and so the sports were held in Lower Close Flowers, a field halfway up Little Somerford Hill which belonged to Colonel Brassey (later Sir Hugh Brassey). The field was suitable because part of it was fairly flat. Colonel Brassey kindly removed his horses from the field for the occasion.

Parental help was enlisted to set up the field. Tapes were strung on lines of metal posts to indicate a small track area which had been especially mown so that we would not be tripping over tussocks of grass. Clear lanes had also been marked out. Since we were a small school, only about twenty-eight children in total, most of the children had to take part in several races and some of the older ones had to compete in five or six. Excited children, who had been practising for weeks, were eager to show off their skills and crowded round their teachers who were giving out coloured bands to denote the different age groups. Quite a few parents had come along to help or watch their children.

The races were held according to age with the sack races for the infants held first, so this year I had to wait until it was my turn. Coarse hessian sacks with the logo of Wiltshire Farmers had been brought out from the small shed where the physical education equipment was stored. These were handed out to the smallest children who were five or six years of age. Some of the sacks were too big and had to be turned down at the top. Others had been chewed by mice since the previous year and were full of holes. A few of these had to be discarded. The children were helped into their sacks and lined up eagerly on the starting line. A parent blew a whistle and off they went, bouncing down the track with great enthusiasm in big hops, encouraged by parental shouts of encouragement. One child tripped up and fell flat, but was quickly helped up and ushered on their way. After a few minutes the parents applauded the winner and the children stepped out of their sacks and handed them over to their teacher. Soon it was our turn. My sack was motheaten and musty and not as roomy as some and I had to make a big effort to jump forwards instead of jumping on the spot. the children in roomy sacks it seemed to me had an advantage of freer movement. I came last!

Next was the Egg and Spoon race. Some of the eggs were china ones of the sort placed under hens to encourage them to lay and were on loan from parents. Others were hard boiled hens' eggs. No sensible villager would waste eggs, especially as food rationing was still a recent memory. Hard boiled eggs could be picked up if they were dropped and at the end of the races given to children to eat. Children were lined up in their heats and first spoons and then eggs were handed out. Holding our loaded spoons at waist height, we had to run down the track without dropping our eggs with parents waiting at the finishing line to record the winners.

There were short sprinting races for both the infants and juniors and then the older children took part in three-legged races which had to be run in pairs. Each pair of children having a leg tied to their partner's nearest leg with a scarf. Then with their arms around one another's shoulders they had to run down the track. This was followed by the Wheelbarrow race, again run in pairs. One child got down on all fours and their partner picked up their legs and held them just above their own knee height as they would the handles of a wheelbarrow. Like this, they moved as fast as they could to the finishing line. Copying them, I ran down the track clutching Angela's ankles and she moved so fast walking on her hands that I had to run my hardest to keep up.

These races were followed by a relay race in teams of three with bean bags being passed from person to person at each stage. By this time more parents had arrived as it was nearly the end of the afternoon and of course the highlight was the Mothers' Race. Our mother was always at work and so was unable to take part, but there were quite a few mothers who were keen to participate. They were very competitive and kicked off their shoes in order to run more easily in bare feet. The whistle blew and they were off to cheers and claps and hurtled down the track laughing. One very tall mother had long legs and was able to reach the finish several yards ahead of her rivals.

Glasses of squash were handed out to thirsty children as the clearing up began. Sacks were folded ready to go back to their shelf. Tape was gathered in and coiled up and metal posts removed. Children were lined up ready to return to school to change out of their shorts and daps (North-Wiltshire children call their plimsolls *daps*). A final check of the field was made by parents to make absolutely sure that there was no litter or anything else which might be a danger to the horses who normally grazed there. Our next day's English lesson involved writing letters of thanks to Colonel Brassey for the use of his field.

Yew Tree Farm
(by kind permission of Oliver Jones Davies)

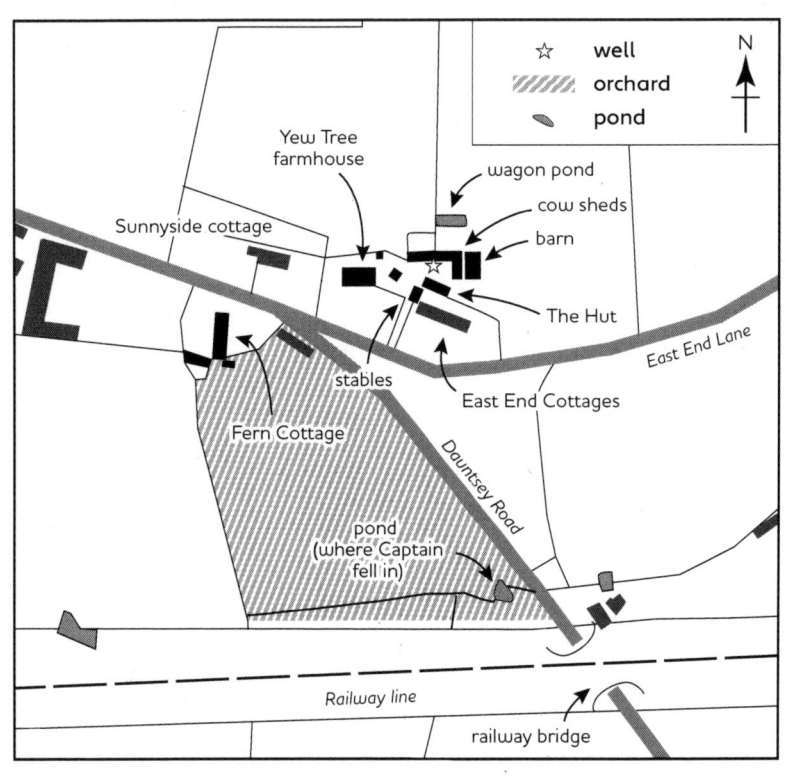

Plan of Yew Tree Farm (not to scale)

CHAPTER 8

THE HUT

I WAS ALWAYS fascinated on the rare occasions when I was allowed to go into The Hut, a large single-storey farm building in the yard at Yew Tree Farm. Its foundations were of brick but most of the part above ground was made of weather proofed overlapping wooden planks, with large double doors at one end.

This was where the Reeves kept all their farm tools and a few other things besides. It was probably purpose built and its inside was studded with hooks and nails so that tools could be hung on the walls. All the tools were carefully cleaned and the metal parts greased or wiped with an oily rag to prevent rust, then the tools were hung up in their allotted places.

On the end wall were rows of wooden rakes for turning hay. These included a half-size rake which was once brought out for me to use. It had been made so that the Reeve children could help with the harvest. Wooden rakes are rather heavy so the smaller one would have been essential if the Reeve children were to learn harvesting skills. There were also one or two modern metal rakes for the front lawn. Then came the forks and pitchforks, the latter having two sharp thin prongs which turned up at the ends. The pitchforks were used for tossing sheaves of corn or piles of hay onto a wagon or rick. There were several spades and shovels alongside the forks and one spade had a longer narrower blade and was possibly used for digging ditches or a narrow trench for planting crops. Their blade edges gleamed in the half light of The Hut.

A little further along were the scythes. There were three and these were almost certainly made to measure by the village blacksmith. Cutting hay or corn is heavy, relentless work and having one's own scythe would enable a person to work more quickly and comfortably, and build up a smooth rhythm of cutting which could be carried on for hours. One of the scythes was much smaller and lighter than the others and again was probably made for the Reeve boys to use when they were first learning to cut corn. Other farm workers who were hired to help with the harvest would bring their own scythe and sharpening tool with them.

On many occasions I had the pleasure of watching John Reeve, our neighbour, using a scythe to cut long grass at the edge of his garden. He would draw the scythe through the grass in a smooth rhythm that was almost mesmerising to watch, stopping now and again to hone the blade. He would sharpen the blades of shears and bill hooks using a large sharpening stone suspended on a frame and turned with a handle, but his scythe blade was always sharpened by hand with a small whetstone.

On another wall of The Hut were the smaller tools: several different sized bill hooks for hedging, and sickles for cutting nettles and brambles. At the far end was an old horse drawn plough, a row of wheelbarrows neatly upended and metal feeders for hens or ducks. Several wood and metal sieves hung on the wall next to the yard brushes and further along was the wooden yoke for carrying two buckets of water, or milk or pig swill at one go. Of course, Victorian buckets were much heavier than the modern aluminium or plastic buckets of today. The yoke had a shaped wooden piece to fit across the neck and shoulders and from each end hung a short chain with a hook at the end. Buckets would be suspended from each hook, allowing the carrier to be evenly balanced and less likely to spill the contents of the buckets as well as distributing the weight evenly across the person's shoulders. I have several times seen Ernest Reeve using the yoke to carry two large buckets of water.

Near the doors of The Hut were three large wooden barrels, pale golden in colour and hooped with metal. These had clearly been bought when newly made and were so lovely I could have admired them for hours. They were illuminated by a beam of sunlight from the open doors and their edges were polished smooth by years of someone rubbing against them as they scooped out a measure of corn. These still contained some corn and bran left over from when the Reeves owned Captain the carthorse. Some of the corn was fed to John Reeve's chickens when he lived at Sunnyside, the cottage next to Yew Tree Farm.

I wish the Hut had been preserved; it was a real museum piece, a relic of a bygone age. Many of those tools would no longer be used today. With the advent of tractors and modern harvesting equipment much of the relentless back-breaking work of Victorian farming was no longer necessary, and in many ways this was a very good thing, but sometimes I felt sad to see so many beautiful things, previously essential, but now no longer used.

CHAPTER 9

THE WELL

KATE REEVE told me that when they moved into Yew Tree farm in 1921, there was very little water on the farm, apart from one or two ponds. Mr Alfred Reeve, Kate's father, was anxious that they should have a reliable water supply so he enquired about finding a good dowser. A dowser is someone who uses a divining rod to find underground water.

There was a cattle market in Devizes where the Reeves bought and sold animals and this is probably where Alfred Reeve heard about the dowser. The dowser lived near Devizes and drove out to Little Somerford in his pony trap. The divining rod he used was a forked hazel twig in the shape of a Y. The dowser spent a whole day walking all over Yew Tree Farm with his dowsing rod. He held the two forked ends of the stick in his hands and pointed the single piece upwards at an angle as he walked, following the lines of underground streams.

At the end of the day, he pointed to a spot in the farmyard and said, 'There is where you need to put your Well.'

Apparently, it was a spot where two underground streams crossed. This meant that if one stream stopped flowing, the other would ensure the water supply for the farm. The dowser also told the Reeves how deep the well needed to be. The well was sunk at that spot and it was one hundred feet deep, following the dowser's advice. For the next sixty years it provided water for the farm and never ever went dry. An engine at the top of the well pumped the water up when it was needed and a special hose was connected to the engine.

The steady hum of the engine could be heard every milking time when water was being used to cool the milk churns or hose down the cow shed when the cows had departed to their field. We were warned against going too near when the well was open and our black cat, Monty – who was chief mouser at Yew Tree when their own tortoiseshell cat Amos died – nearly fell into the well when she took a look to see if any mice were down there. Luckily, David Gleed, the farm man, just managed to grab her and after that he put a metal grid over the open well head when it was in use. When not in use it was covered by a stone slab with a large metal ring embedded in it so that it could be lifted when the water was needed.

Little Somerford Garage c.1945. George Higgs proprietor is on right.
The little building on the right is the old Victorian village Post Office
(by kind permission of Nigel King and Geoffrey Snelgrove)

CHAPTER 10

THE OLD FORGE

THERE WAS NEVER a forge when we lived at Little Somerford, the blacksmith's sons had turned the old forge building into a garage and to be fair to them, this was the only way to make a living after the increased availability of motor cars and the advent of modern farming methods after the Second World War. Most farmers no longer used carthorses and although farming continued to involve hard physical work, modern machines such as tractors, hay tedders to turn hay in the fields and baling machines replaced a great deal of the hard back-breaking work of crop production which had previously been a fact of farming life.

Our elderly neighbours, the Reeves, often talked to me about the old forge. They described the heat of the fire, the sparks flying from the anvil as a horseshoe was hammered into shape and the smells of coal and metal and horses, together with the singeing smell as the horseshoe was fitted. William and John Reeve used to take their carthorses to be shod there and John Reeve told me that the blacksmith did not like too many people in the forge when a horse was being shod, just one person to stand at the horse's head. Also, being used to working outside on their farm, he found the forge too hot and was always glad to get out into the open air. All the tools in The Hut in their farmyard – the scythes, bill hooks and sickles – would all have been made by the village blacksmith.

Most importantly of all, the blacksmith would ensure that carthorses, without which the farmers could not have ploughed their fields or gathered their harvest, would be well shod. The blacksmith had to be strong, with an affinity for horses and a wide knowledge of their trade. They had to be of calm temperament to deal with the heavy horses and apply the new horseshoes with a steady and sure hand, as well as making wonderful hand-made tools which would last a lifetime and beyond. These tools were no less works of art than anything on display in museums.

THE GARAGE

THE GARAGE as we knew it replaced the old forge. The former forge building itself was used for repairing cars, and they also sold fuel. It was run by George and Alfie Higgs whose father used to be the village black-smith. They both worked on cars brought in for repair, but it was mostly George who dealt with customers. He always seemed a calm, happy, friendly man who wore a long, light brown coat for his work. He had silvery-white hair when we knew him and whistled softly to himself as he helped the customers who wanted fuel. His brother, Alfie was larger in build and had dark brown hair. At that time the garage proprietor served customers and put petrol in their cars for them, instead of the self-service we have these days.

I was once allowed to look in the old forge building and George and Alfie pointed out where the fire used to be and where the anvil stood. The building was situated at right angles to the road so that there would be room for horses to be tied up outside awaiting their turn to be shod. Next to it nowadays, a modern, galvanised iron shed painted a dark grey housed the small goods sold by the garage such as bicycle tyres, lights and batteries. This was where the shop counter and till were.

The three tall petrol pumps had Shell-shaped logos on the top and in the dusk these resembled people. They were lit up when the garage was open in the evening.

THE MODERN FORGE

NOWADAYS A FORGE does exist in Little Somerford, but on a different site, on land formerly owned by the Reeve family which, I am sure, would have pleased them greatly. When I knew it over sixty years ago, the building, now the forge, was an old milking parlour, dairy, stable and three cart bays which were once part of a small farm. They formed a mostly open fronted L-shape round two sides of a small paddock where bullocks were kept for a few months until they were big enough to be sold.

The Hollow Oak (right) in the snow
(by kind permission of Trevor House)

CHAPTER 11

TREES

THE HOLLOW OAK

THE FIRST TIME I was allowed out to play around the village was when I was six years old. Nigel from Street Farm came to call for M, and I begged to go with them. They promised to look after me and we walked down The Street and then turned up the footpath by the side of the churchyard. Nigel knew where there was an owl's nest and he wanted to show us. Behind the Old Rectory was a large field sloping up the gentle hill behind. It was a beautiful field. At one side was a small coppice where there were a few hazel bushes. On the ground were a number of hazelnut shells with neat holes nibbled in the sides. These showed where dormice had been feeding. In the centre of the field was a large and ancient oak tree of massive girth.

This venerable tree may have been pollarded during the earlier part of its life as its trunk was knobbled and gnarled where branches had been lopped years before. The tree, owing to its situation, had at one time probably been the victim of a lightning strike as its centre was blackened and charred where it had been completely burnt out, leaving just the outside wood and bark which were still alive and supporting several large branches at the top of the trunk. These were in leaf and gave it an air of grandeur, a symbol of endurance against the ravages of time. There was an arched hole at its base enabling children to creep in and peer up at the leafy canopy above. Nigel, M and myself all stood inside and there was still room for a couple more small children.

The owls were luckily not in residence, so quickly we were able to climb up to see the nest. We did not touch it, and only spent a minute up there in case the owls returned. Hastily we scrambled down and left the tree to the owls. We visited this tree on a number of occasions over the next few years, just to admire it and marvel at its survival. Sadly, it has now disappeared and is just a memory for the older villagers.

JOHN REEVE'S OAK TREE

THERE WERE TWO other oak trees which I liked. The relatively young oak which stands opposite the Somerford Arms, in what was a small paddock next to old farm buildings, was planted by John Reeve, a farmer's son, who at that time lived at Street Farm. He told me how, on his sixth birthday, 25 September 1893, his father, Alfred Reeve, had allowed him to plant the tree as a birthday treat. He and his father had walked down the road, his father carrying the oak sapling with its roots wrapped in a piece of sacking, in one hand and a bucket of water in the other. John walked beside him carrying a spade. His father dug the hole and John removed the sacking and placed the sapling in the hole and Mr Reeve held the tree upright while John filled it in and then his father showed him how to firm the soil and water the tree. John Reeve was very proud of this tree and kept an eye on it for the rest of his life. It was lovely for him as an old man to recall this precious memory, and whenever I revisit the village I always admire John Reeve's oak tree and remember him fondly because we knew him very well.

The other oak tree I loved was on the far side of the field from John Reeve's oak. Set in the hedge between Old Cousens and Little Nurnalls fields it was also hollow, though not burnt out and nowhere near as old and venerable as the huge oak near the Old Rectory. This one too had an oval hole, like a small doorway, where small children could slip inside and it was hollowed in such a way that it was like a tiny room, having a ledge of wood on one side like a seat and an extra hollow on the opposite side like a tiny grate. For a young child it was perfect for playing houses in and I visited it on a number of occasions when I was six. When Kate Reeve asked me why I had been walking over her field, I told her about the tree and she smiled and said that she and her sister used to play houses there too in the early 1900s. She seemed really pleased that the tree was being played in again.

At one corner of our kitchen garden overlooking the road was a huge clump of five magnificent elm trees. These were beautiful in all weathers and I admired them often. Sadly, during the late 1960s, they became victims of Dutch Elm disease; as did the tall and stately elm growing beside the gateway to the Reeve's orchard, just past our house. I remember John Reeve saying that he had known and admired that tree by the orchard all his life and that he would miss it when it was cut down. Soon Dutch Elm disease had ravaged all the familiar hedgerows and those who loved trees were bereft. I used to stand in Little Nurnalls field and admire the village below, the houses half hidden by the elm trees. There were beautiful elms in many of the hedgerows all around, but after the impact of Dutch Elm Disease there were hardly any elm trees left and from Nurnalls you could see for miles. The dreadful tree beetle had ravaged the whole of the Dauntsey Vale.

CAMP STOOLS

'COME AND MAKE a camp,' suggested my friend Wendy when I was invited to play when I was about ten. 'There's a really good tree in a field, it's not far.'

We crossed the road and cut across a field until we reached a large pollarded ash in the hedge. I did not normally play in those fields as there were other fields much closer to home. We often made camps in pollarded trees. They were normally not too high to climb, usually about eight or nine feet above ground. From our perch we could get a good view of the landscape round about and comment on neighbours passing by on the road. We took sandwiches up there and it was fun to be able to see everything that was going on, but not be seen ourselves.

Since the ash tree was pollarded, there was a flattish central section surrounded by branches and we soon found our way up. After admiring the view and fixing Wendy's rope ladder to suitable branches to provide easier access we set about making the tree house more to our liking. We decided that the green grassy area at the base of the tree would make a good picnic area if we had some seating. Looking over into the next field I saw some sawn up sections of tree trunk which would be perfect as camp stools. I climbed down, opened the gate into the field next door and rolled two sections of tree trunk to the base of our tree and set them upright before closing the field gate. We were just admiring our new picnic area when Mr Berry, the farmer rushed up and demanded to know what we were doing with his logs. I hastily explained that we were hoping to use them as seats for our camp.

'We...ll,' came the reply, 'I 'spose you're not doin' any harm. Make sure you put them back when you've finished with them – this isn't my field!'

I was shocked, I had automatically assumed they were both his fields and by rights he should have been furious at us removing his logs to someone else's land. I was often amazed at the kindness and tolerance of the older villagers towards the village children as long as we weren't doing anything considered to be deliberate wrongdoing.

CHESTNUTS

THERE WERE other trees which were of interest to us children. Outside the church on a raised grass verge next to the footpath were three lovely chestnut trees. In spring, a few of the sticky buds were brought into the village school for display on the Nature Table. In September they were the first port of call for children in search of conkers. Usually the children passing that way on their way to school would secure the best conkers, so the rest of us would rush to check fallen conkers underneath the two chestnut trees behind the village hall. When we were a little older, we would have expeditions to a huge chestnut tree across the fields on the Dauntsey Road. The biggest conkers which were much sought after would be found there.

One day my mother became very cross at finding piles of conkers around the house where we had left them. She threw them all out onto the garden, but to her consternation they started rooting and she had to pull them all up and burn them on the garden bonfire.

John Reeve's oak, planted 25 September 1893
(image by Ceri Vyner, with kind permission of Hector Cole)

CHAPTER 12

THE GATEWAY

THE OLD WEATHERED wooden gate mottled with patches of yellow and off-white lichen, guarded the entrance to the farmyard at Street Farm over sixty years ago. The gateway itself was lovely with grassy verges on either side and umbels of cow parsley growing near the hedge and dandelions, buttercups, forget-me-nots and clover growing by the wooden gateposts.

On one side was the great wagon shed, a double shed built of wood to house the great hay wains used to bring in the harvest in the days of horse power. Flower and Violet were the Reeves' carthorses back then and it was their job to pull the great wagons and bring the harvest home. At the top of the shed was the pigeon loft and at one time Mr Maidment kept racing pigeons there. I did not like passing the wagon shed in the dark. The blackness of the darkness there was impenetrable and any imaginative child would find it a fearful experience. There were no hay wains in it when we knew it, for the Reeves had taken them when they moved to Yew Tree Farm just up the road. Instead, it just housed the grey Ford tractor and the old pony trap which the Reeves had left behind because they no longer had a pony. This, Ernest told me many years later, was a pity because the trap would have come in handy during the days of petrol rationing during the Second World War.

'But we'd sold the pony, see, before we moved and the trap wasn't any use without a pony,' said Ernest.

Alongside the farm gate was the mounting block. Built of Cotswold stone, it had five steps on the road side of it leading up to the flat platform at the top which was about five feet square. When the Reeves lived at Street farm, their pony would be harnessed to the trap and the trap backed up to the mounting block on the farmyard side. The Reeve ladies in their long Victorian or Edwardian dresses would go out of the farm gate, climb the steps of the mounting block and be able to open the small door in the back of the pony trap and step straight into it and sit down. One of the Reeve men, usually Charles, would then drive them to their destination.

Kate Reeve told me that she never drove the trap herself as she was too nervous. She went out in the trap with her sister Nellie (really her niece, but the Reeve children were brought up to regard her as their sister) and the pony nearly bolted when it was spooked by something, so after that they always asked one of their brothers to drive them. When the Reeves were young – in the 1890s – two people driving a trap along the main Malmesbury to Swindon road, just past the top of Little Somerford Hill, were killed when their pony bolted and they were thrown out of the trap onto the road.

When M and I played at Street Farm with Nigel Maidment, we sometimes played with the trap, wheeling it out of the cart shed, backing it up to the mounting block and climbing the steps to get in, just as the Reeves would have done and pretending we had a pony between the shafts and were going for a drive.

The mounting block was at that time used as a stand for the silver-coloured milk churns and its height was of great assistance to the dairyman who collected the heavy churns after milking twice a day and unloaded the empty ones from his lorry. The regular clang of the churns being collected or delivered was a familiar background noise in our lives.

Late one afternoon in early summer, M and I were waving to Nigel Maidment as we left Street Farm after an afternoon spent there playing and helping around the farmyard. As we turned out of the farmyard we encountered about twenty fireflies near the mounting block. We were amazed as we had never seen them before and called Nigel back to have a look. Dusk was beginning to fall and the fireflies glowed as they flew around. I managed to catch one in my cupped hands and was surprised to see a small black beetle with a cream stripe and no light coming from it at all. I released it and after a few seconds I saw its back end glowing as it flew beside its companions. We watched them entranced before reluctantly heading home to tell our mother about them.

Our mother had never seen a firefly and the following day when she visited Yew Tree Farm she told Kate Reeve about them in a slightly disbelieving tone.

'Oh yes!' said Kate, 'we always saw fireflies there by

the gateway. We never saw them anywhere else, but we always saw them there.'

The road verges began to be sprayed with pesticides soon after that and sadly, I never saw the fireflies again, but our encounter with them remains a very special memory.

Street Farm from the road, 2023

CHAPTER 13

PETRICHOR AND OTHER SMELLS

THE HEAVENS OPENED and the rain poured down in torrents onto the dry ground. The soil surface was pummelled into a porridge-like consistency by the relentless rain which puddled onto the dried clayey soil. Then the monsoon gradually subsided and settled into a steady drizzle. Rain poured into the cracks of the dried earth. It flowed in the gutters, gurgled in the drains and raced along the ditches. Although it continued to fall, it was a soft, gentle rain, soaking the ground beneath but not destroying the plants and trees. The flowers relaxed, opening their leaves to take in this sustenance and everything was refreshed. Gradually the rain stopped and water vapour rose gently from the ground bearing with it the fresh scents of the garden.

Petrichor, the scent of rain on warm earth after dry weather, was something I always looked forward too, something that always drew me into the garden. It is the scent of the earth itself, rich and dark and mysterious, with a distant memory of compost and vegetation. It was a background scent to the heady perfume of phlox and lavender, honeysuckle and roses. Not the modern hybrid roses, but the small, heavily-scented Victorian musk roses with their clusters of delicious smelling, blush white flowers, grown as standards by some keen gardener of yesteryear; probably Mr Sloper who lived in our cottage before us.

In the background was the smell of freshly cut grass, one of the best of all scents and only surmounted by the wonderful smell of sweet meadow hay. On warm summer evenings this was intensified by the perfume from the night-scented stocks in the border and the Albertine roses that grew over the hedge. I would breathe deep of the scented evening air, still holding some of the warmth of the day while listening to the thrush sing singing from the old walnut tree in the orchard.

Petrichor! It was something so special that I once wrote an essay about it for my English homework, but I did not know the word then, not until our English teacher told me, I only knew what it meant to me.

Then there was the scent of herbs: rosemary and mint, thyme and golden oregano, sage and parsley. I would pluck a few leaves and crush them between my fingers, and hold them to my nose, to breathe in their sweet odour. Leaves from the currant bushes too, had a strong scent like the geraniums my mother had planted in the old stone sink near the gate and which made me wrinkle my nose as the scent was too powerful for my taste.

Japanese honeysuckle with its deep cream and pink flowers grew rampantly up the back wall of the cottage and its delicate but distinct scent delighted me. Time after time, as a small child, I gathered the flowers and added them to an old empty bottle with a small amount of water. After sealing the bottle with a cork I would leave it in the cool wash-house for two weeks. I hoped for a bottle of beautiful scent, but instead was disappointed to find rotting flowers in rancid water. How I longed to replicate the delicious scent of the honeysuckle.

The smell of a garden bonfire, wood and ash and burning vegetation hung in the air and even now the scent of a bonfire transports me back down the years and fills me with nostalgia. I loved the autumnal scents too, especially quinces, a glorious smell. Two or three quinces placed in a bowl on the kitchen table scented the whole room and their wonderful soft mustard-yellow colour cheered the heart. The scent of autumn was always a mixture of quinces and apples, rotting leaves and a hint of frost combined with woodsmoke. Frost and snow could be smelled in the air, you did not need to see your breath clouding the air in front of your face, or look up at the stars shimmering coldly in a clear night sky, you only had to close your eyes and smell to know of a pending frost or snowstorm.

A FEW YEARS ago a family friend came to stay, bringing with them a bottle of Chianti which they had bought in Italy. That evening I had one sip of that glorious wine and I was instantly transported back in time, when as a small child of eight I stood in the grass of the Reeves' orchard behind our house, helping John Reeve to pick up windfall apples. The Tom Putt cider apples, red and juicy, smelled and tasted exactly like the Chianti wine. I was fighting back tears at the coincidence, such is the power of scent and taste. I have drunk several Chianti wines since, trying to track down that elusive scent, but never had one that so closely matched the taste and smell of the Tom Putt apples.

Another nostalgic scent is the rather bitter and acrid scent of hawthorn. Time and again I walked up East End Lane just to smell the hawthorn and admire the tiny pinky-white clusters of flowers, but it is the smell I remember, catching in my throat, a smell which both attracted and repelled me in equal measure. It is supposed to be the smell of death itself, but it brings back so many memories that I cannot be without the scent of hawthorn in any spring.

✝

TO THE GLORY OF GOD AND IN MEMORY OF
THE LIVES SACRIFICED AND SERVICE RENDERED TO
THEIR KING AND COUNTRY IN THE GREAT WAR 1914-1919
BY THE FOLLOWING MEN OF THIS PARISH.

2ND LIEUT. R.SIMMONS. SGT. W.SLY. CPLS. W.BAILEY, P.WALL.
PTES. D.BARNES, G.HURST, J.SLY, W.STRANGE.
PTES. J.SPARROW, J.WAKELING, TPR. C.PINNELL.

R.I.P.

2ND LIEUT. A.MORTIMER, SGT. MJR. H.JEFFERIES, W.TEAGLE
CPLS. W.STONEHAM, C.JEFFERIES, L.CPL. A.HARFORD.
GNRS. C.BARNES, W.BARNES, H.PINNELL.
GNRS. W.PINNELL, J.REEVE, J.WOODMAN.
TPRS. R.PORTLOCK, W.SCOTT. DVR. S.CARTER.
DVR. W.PARSLOE, SAPPER. A.PONTING. PTE. A.BAILEY.
PTES. RY BARNES, T.BARNES, RD BARNES.
PTES. A.BAKER, T.BROOME, E.CARTER.
PTES. F.CARTER, ED CARTER, W.CHIVERS, C.DAY.
PTES. C.FRY, G.HALL, R.HARFORD, F.JEFFERIES.
PTES. H.PONTING, W.REEVE, J.STRANGE, C.SCOTT.
PTES. E.SLY, A.STONEHAM, D.STONEHAM.
PTES. E.STONEHAM, W.SLOPER, R.THOMAS.
PTES. G.WAKELING, L.WAKELING, W.WAKELING.
PTES. A.WEBB, P.WOODWARD, J.BYE.

THIS TABLET WAS ERECTED AND AN ORGAN PLACED
IN THE CHURCH BY THE PARISHIONERS.

EDWARD MORTIMER   W.R.TEAGLE, A.F.HISCOCK
RECTOR.   CHURCHWARDENS.

WEBB.CHIPP'H

Village war memorial, Little Somerford Church

CHAPTER 14

THE THIRD LIGHT

THE VETERANS of both World Wars had a special status in the village. They were immensely respected and admired. Their rank was not considered to be of such importance, but it was their service and where they served that was important and the collective acknowledgement of their service.

The First World War Memorial in little Somerford church records not only the eleven poor men who never returned to the village, but the forty-seven other men who served. The memorial gives their rank and records the gratitude that was felt throughout the whole country.

I noticed that William and John Reeve, our close neighbours, were especially respected, having taken part in action at Ypres, Passchendaele and on the Somme in WW1. They were both in the Royal Garrison Artillery. John Reeve's rank is given as Gunner, and William's as Private, but they both worked together in an artillery team. They were also both very experienced at looking after heavy horses, having taken responsibility for helping with the carthorses on the family farm since boyhood. When John Reeve died in 1969, a near neighbour, Commander Jenkins, himself an extremely brave man who commanded destroyers in WW2, called on the Reeves to give his condolences and requested the honour of giving the Address. He, in particular, felt that he was able to do justice to the history of such a man.

Ernest Reeve, John's youngest brother, was still a schoolboy at the start of the First world War. As soon as he was old enough he tried to enlist, but when he attended a medical examination at Devizes in 1917, he was turned away on health grounds. He was short sighted and this would have put him at a great disadvantage on the battlefield at that time. Many years later he told me of his disappointment at not being able to join up. He had tried his best to do his duty for his country. No doubt he was subjected to pointed remarks by villagers who were unaware of his efforts to enlist or of any medical condition which might prevent him taking an active part in the war. I, however, was pleased that Ernest was unable to go and fight in 1917 and I told him why. William and John Reeve both returned safely from the First World War, but it is extremely unlikely that a third brother would have had the same luck.

I OFTEN STOOD on the sidelines at village events and watched the people around me.

On one occasion I observed four of the older village men who had gathered together. These four men were well known to their companions and greeted each other warmly. One man immediately drew out a packet of Woodbine cigarettes from his jacket pocket and proceeded to hand them round. Then he reached into his inside pocket for his cigarette lighter, flicked it open and spun the wheel to light the flame. His face was briefly illuminated in a soft glow as it flared into life. He offered the lighter in turn to his companions. They leaned in towards the flame to light their cigarettes and their faces were heightened into chiaroscuros by the flickering flame. Then they drew back, drawing the smoke into their lungs appreciatively before removing their cigarettes from their mouths in order to blow away the smoke and talk.

However, the third man quickly removed his cigarette from his mouth before it could be lit and said in some consternation: 'I can't take that, *it's the third light!'*

'Oh, sorry!' replied the man with the lighter, 'I'll start again.'

He closed the lighter, then opened it again to flick the wheel and light it again before offering it to his companion who bent his head towards the lighter and then drew back in obvious relief at avoiding the third light.

I was puzzled by this and told my mother about it later. She explained that these men were veterans who had fought in World War One, when any flickering light in a trench on the front line would show our enemy soldiers where our troops were. The third light was considered very unlucky because by the light of a match our soldiers could be located, if the match was then offered to someone else an enemy could find a target, and by the third light shoot someone dead. These men had all fought in WW1 on the front line, when a small flame could be not just a light for a cigarette, but a matter of life and death.

It is interesting that over forty years after the end of the First World War the old soldiers were still anxious to avoid any possible bad luck and careful to observe the rule of the third light.

CHAPTER 15

MISS BOND AND
OLD FLYNN

MISS SHEILA BOND lived at Malthouse Farm up East End Lane. She farmed there with her father and brother, but after her brother moved away and her father died, she found the heavy work on the farm too much so she gave up farming and opened a dog boarding kennels instead.

Miss Bond was a shy person, very quiet and extremely hardworking. She was slim and small boned with bobbed brown hair. She usually dressed in trousers and top with a fawn coloured duffle coat over these if the weather was cold, as she was often walking dogs.

Miss Bond loved animals, especially dogs, and basset hounds in particular. She was hardly ever seen around the village unless she had her basset hounds, Benny and Penny, with her. When eventually one of the dogs died, it was replaced with an almost identical dog and given the same name. There were three sets of Bennys and Pennys while we lived at Somerford!

Eventually, Miss Bond found living at Malthouse Farm rather lonely so she sold it and moved to a modern house on the Vale Leaze housing estate. Where she continued to live for some years.

At one time Miss Bond had a donkey which kept escaping from its field. Whatever she did, she could not stop this donkey getting out. She said that this was because it wanted company. Luckily, Colonel Brassey had a donkey, their much loved family pet Old Flynn, on which the Brassey children had learned to ride. Miss Bond's donkey would escape from her field, trot down the lane and on down the street to Old Flynn's field and nuzzle him over the gate. After being taken home numerous times, the donkey would always return to Old Flynn and so was put in the field with him and they kept each other company for several years.

OLD FLYNN

FOR AS LONG as I could remember, Old Flynn, the brown donkey, had cropped the grass in his field opposite Manor Farm and would wait at the gate to be fed handfuls of grass by passing children, even though he had plenty of grass of his own.

On one occasion I had a large yellow quince in my bag and I waved this at Old Flynn to bring him to the gate so that I could say hello to him. Quinces have a delectable smell and Old Flynn came rushing over immediately hoping for a treat. Fortunately for him I was much too fond of him to feed him sour quince which would have given him colic. He had to make do with grass, but Old Flynn did not forget and eyed me with suspicion after that. He would not come over to the gate to greet me thereafter. I was the person who had denied him a delicious treat.

*The old barn opposite Manor Farm. The gateway is where
Old Flynn the donkey waited to be fed by passers-by
(by kind permission of Arlene Bishop)*

CHAPTER 16

INSIDE YEW TREE FARMHOUSE

YEW TREE FARM when we first knew it could not have changed much since Victorian times or earlier. The Reeves did have a fairly modern freestanding electric oven, probably 1940s in date, in a corner of the kitchen, but until 1958 the old copper kettle was boiled over the coal fire which had a hob on the right-hand side. The kettle was lifted onto a hook hanging from the tackle at the side of the chimney and swung over the hottest part of the fire and then lifted off when the water was hot and used to fill the brown teapot. Then the kettle was placed on the hob to keep warm.

A pine table and elm chairs furnished the room. The floor was of old stone flags then, with a small rag rug in front of the hearth. There was no sink in the kitchen until a certain amount of modernisation was done in 1958. Washing up and also some washing was done in an enamel bowl at the kitchen table. A stone sink, together with a pump were outside under a sheltered area about three feet wide where the roof overhung. It was open to the elements otherwise. Water was pumped by hand either into the sink itself, or into a bucket for household use. There was a large stone-flagged room next to the kitchen which was used to store vegetables and eggs and it just had a long pine table against one wall near the back door and a store cupboard against another wall. On the table, apart from the eggs in their grey egg box, were several wicker baskets ready to hand for anyone about to pick vegetables or fruit from the garden.

Beyond this room was a tiny room known as the cellar. You had to step down two steps to enter it. It backed onto the dairy and was very cool. Milk and cream and cheese were stored here, together with any other perishable food. There was no refrigerator. Unopened jars of jam were stored all over the ground floor of the house, including in the case of the grandfather clock which stood in the hall.

Built onto the kitchen was the old wash house which had a copper in one corner and contained various laundry tools such as a mangle for squeezing water out of washed items and the big wicker basket which was used for transporting washing to and from the washing line in the paddock nearby. The large butter churn was also kept here. I remember my mother being given a pat of butter which Jane Reeve had made that day. I must only have been about three years old then, as Jane Reeve died when I was five. I remember tasting the butter later and it was very good.

The Reeves had an old-fashioned iron too. Kate Reeve would not use electricity unless she had to. The iron she used was hollow inside with a little door in the body of it. Kate opened the tiny door and put in hot coals from the fire. After a minute Kate spat on the sole plate on the iron and if it sizzled, it showed that the iron was hot enough and she proceeded to iron several garments as she chatted to my mother. My mother was asking how the iron worked and I observed with interest. This was probably a Victorian iron which the Reeves had used all their lives. Kate had three sizes of old irons, the lighter smoothing irons being used to iron more delicate fabrics.

The furniture polish Kate used was a bottle of brownish liquid which she had purchased several years before from a gypsy. It contained linseed oil and did leave a beautiful shine when it was wiped on wooden furniture. This polish lasted for years and I used to use it to polish furniture at Yew Tree Farm when I was a teenager.

During the first half of the 1950s, the Reeve women made all their bread and cakes, jams and marmalade, pies and puddings. Their farm supplied them with milk and cream. After her sisters died, Kate continued to do as much baking as she could until arthritis prevented her.

The living room had a large Victorian oak table with bulbous legs. This table was always covered by a red chenille table cloth which had a bobbly fringe along its edges. There were three armchairs and a Windsor chair next to the table. A chaise-longue stood along one wall and a large bureau desk stood in another corner. On either side of the fireplace were four deep cupboards, two on each side. China and vases were kept on one side, glasses and a tin of biscuits were kept on the other side to be handy for use after supper. An open fire burned in the grate in cold weather and there was a brass fender and fire guard as well as a fire side companion-set of poker, hand shovel and small brush. The fire surround was black marble with a wide mantle-piece above which was an oval mirror with a gilt frame.

Above the chaise-longue was a small wall-mounted bookcase with about a dozen books in it, including Mrs Beeton's *Everyday Cookery*. I was always intrigued by another book entitled: *Enquire Within Upon Everything*. There was also a wartime handbook and a small book on first aid. There were two or three classics by Dickens and Sir Walter Scott, but the Reeves were not readers. On the wall was a kitchen clock with a large face. The surround of the clock face was shaped like a flower and the short pendulum was enclosed below the face in a rectangular glass fronted box. I liked this clock because it had a lovely tick. As a teenager, I was sometimes allowed to wind it up. On the walls were two plate type ornaments with a scene in relief.

The door of the living room opened onto a tiled hallway with the front door at one end. The hallway narrowed as it ran beside the staircase until it ended at a door which opened into the back storeroom next to the kitchen. There was a cupboard under the stairs which was now empty, but which, Kate told me, had been used to shelter the Reeve women during the occasional air raids in World War Two. One bomb had apparently dropped in Dauntsey Park, just over a mile away. Also in the hall was a small side table that held the old black telephone, used mainly in emergencies to summon a doctor or vet.

On the opposite side of the hall was the sitting room, although it was not usually used by the Reeves on a daily basis. There were several armchairs in front of the fireplace. On one side of it was an old piano with a pleated silk area across the upright back and two candle brackets fixed on either side of the music stand. The keys were yellowed with age and it clearly had not been played for years. There was a lovely walnut music cabinet with various pieces of music in it. One or two family photos were framed and hung on the walls and these were fascinating to me as I was unable to imagine some of the Reeves as young people, yet here they were, young and in their prime. I felt sad that Ernest, the youngest had never left the family farm and had always had to work very hard without any wages of his own and no days off.

Upstairs there were three bedrooms on the first floor. The main bedroom had a half-tester bed in it and had been used by Mr and Mrs Reeve. Probably all the Reeve children had been born in that bed and some of them died in it! In the second largest bedroom, at the front of the house, was an iron bed with a huge feather mattress. I slept there once when Ernest was in hospital and Kate needed company. On the wide landing was a large chest on chest, an amazing and very grand piece of furniture. Then a narrow staircase led up to two large attics which had been used as bedrooms by some of the Reeve men when they first moved to Yew Tree, and two evacuee boys had slept in one attic during the 1940s. Several dismantled iron beds were set against the walls. Each attic had a small window in each end and the views, towards Sunnyside on one side and up East End Lane on the other, were amazing.

Nellie Reeve (left) and Kate Reeve (right)

CHAPTER 17

ITINERANT VISITORS

OCCASIONAL VISITORS to the village included two tramps who came around two or three times a year. One man did not seem very pleasant and I would suggest now that he probably had mental health problems. We sometimes gave him a sandwich to take away. The other tramp we liked because he was a pleasant chatty man once he got to know the villagers a little. This man had bright red hair and sometimes knocked on the door to ask for a refill of his billy-can. Sometimes he just thrust his arm holding the can through the open living room window if it was a warm summer day. This was quite startling if it was unexpected.

'Can you spare a bit of bread and cheese and refill my billycan?' he'd say. After a few visits he was willing to talk and said that he was a Second World War veteran who had had a bad experience during the war. It had destroyed his trust in society and after being demobbed he had decided that he preferred not to stay in one place, but to travel around. He had a regular route and I know of several other people in the village who gave him tea and sandwiches as we did. I once said to my friend Wendy at school. 'A tramp came to our house on Saturday, we gave him some sandwiches and refilled his billy-can with tea.'

'We gave him sandwiches too!' said Wendy looking surprised.' My mum always gives him sandwiches.'

'So does mine.' I laughed. It was obvious that he consumed one lot of tea and sandwiches and then asked for more so that he had some for later.

Gypsies camped on the wide grass verge of the road near the top of Clay Street during the 1950s. They came in late spring and this stop was one on their regular circuit. The verge there was so wide that I often wondered if it had been a drove road at one time. There were three gypsy caravans, two of which were the traditional ones with canvas roofs stretched over a framework and drawn by ponies. Whether this was one extended family or several we did not know. There were a number of adults and several small children. I never went too near them because they had fierce dogs which barked loudly if anyone went within a few hundred yards of them. They cooked over an open fire and stayed there for two or three weeks before moving on. The gypsy women would walk from house to house selling clothes pegs, round wicker baskets or lucky white heather. My mother did not like to turn them away without buying anything so she usually bought clothes pegs. These were lovely handmade pegs known as dolly pegs because with their oval tops resembling a miniature human head and the forked end resembling legs, they could be dressed by small children and a face drawn on the oval head to represent a doll. I suppose poor children in the past would have played with these if they did not have a doll. The dolly pegs were much more attractive than the spring pegs of today and did not fall apart. The wicker baskets were useful for gathering vegetables or picking blackberries.

CHAPTER 18

CHRISTMAS AT LITTLE SOMERFORD SCHOOL

DURING THE SECOND week of December, the children's growing excitement could no longer be ignored and the school began to prepare for Christmas. Of course, various activities like the planning for the end of term Nativity or craftwork intended for parental Christmas presents had been started long since.

The Infants class was invited into the Big Room, as the Junior classroom was called, and we were carefully divided into groups of five or six children of mixed ages. Each group was given a large cane hoop to decorate. Firstly red or green crepe paper was chosen by each group and our teacher helped cut the bundles of crepe paper; a colourful, wrinkled, stretchy paper into thin strips. Once we had our strips we had to decorate our hoop by twining the strips of crepe paper around it and fixing the end with Sellotape. Eventually all the cane had been covered up and this kept us busy for half an afternoon.

When we came into school the next day we were amazed to find our hoops suspended at intervals from the Big Room ceiling. This was only the start, however, because each child had to design their own decoration to hang from their hoop.

First we had to sketch out our idea on a piece of scrap paper. Then decorations in the form of wobbly stars, balls and bells were carefully drawn on card and cut out. These were coloured and decorated with the addition of shiny stick on stars, spots and glitter. Much of the glitter was spread over our clothes and hands, but nobody minded. Once finished our decorations were attached to a string and tied to our hoops. Before long the room was looking very festive and excitement levels were rising by the hour. We were kept calm by promises of designing our own Christmas cards when we had finished our sums.

We also made presents such as calendars. These were rather clever. Kraft Dairylea cheese boxes – which in those days were round cardboard boxes, about one centimetre deep – had been collected for several weeks and either a base or a lid was given to each pupil. These were designed to be hung up on the wall so we had to paint the inside and outside, and glue small lengths of card inside in the shape of a rudimentary stable: two uprights and a triangular roof. Then we drew, coloured and cut out the shapes of Mary, Joseph and a manger, on which we drew baby Jesus. If we had time, the head of an ox or donkey was also included. These shapes had an extra piece at the foot by which to fold and glue the pieces into position within the stable outline. Finally, a tiny calendar booklet was attached to the foot of the box with Sellotape and ribbon. These were to be given to our parents as Christmas presents. Sometimes we also had handicrafts to take home. Any craft time left over was spent in cutting out complicated snowflake designs on folded white paper and these were stuck on the internal windows between the two classrooms or on the lower panes of the big church style windows at either end of the room.

While our teacher wrote reports or added up marks, we were given the task of making paper chains from coloured strips of gummed paper, whose ends had to be licked or dampened to make the two ends stick together. Our long paper chains were hung around the room in coloured festoons.

The infants practised their carols for our Nativity play and the slightly out of tune but enthusiastic version of the Rocking carol, sung by the infants as 'We will wock you, wock you, wo-ock you', echoed from their side of the partition. Sometimes the Juniors performed a small play in conjunction with the Nativity play, but usually the Juniors were the narrators while the Infants were dressed as angels, Mary, Joseph, shepherds and kings and the carols were sung by the whole school, since there were only about twenty-eight of us in total. It made more sense from the teacher's point of view to have a performance for parents by the older children in the summer as we were less likely to be absent with a cold or influenza. Our Christmas performances were always problematic for teachers then because there were not the inoculations children have today, and so all the children were liable to catch measles, mumps, German measles, and chicken pox as well as the usual colds and influenza, so participation by children in performances between mid-December and Easter could not always be depended upon.

PARTY DAY

THE PENULTIMATE DAY of the Christmas school term was chosen as party day. The party took place in the afternoon and excited children spent half the morning designing Christmas cards or finishing craft work. We had a games lesson in the playground to let off steam and after lunch we moved all the desks to the far end of the room and arranged them in a large horseshoe shape near the Christmas tree. Then we all filed into the Infants' room to listen to a story and rehearse carols for the Nativity play. Next door, a group of mothers were laying out plates of sandwiches, sausage rolls, mini jellies in paper cases and plates of small fancy cakes.

When we returned to the Big Room we were on our best behaviour because parents were there. We sat on the floor at the further end of the room for some party games: musical chairs or pass the parcel. The latter was an exciting game because there were forfeits between the layers of newspaper as well as sweets. For the forfeits we had to hop around the room or sing a verse of *Away in a Manger*. We played Dead Lions and balloon games such as passing a balloon between the knees from person to person. At last it was time for tea and parent helpers encouraged us to have one or two sandwiches before we tucked into the jellies and cakes. Crackers were pulled and we all wore a coloured paper hat and laughed uproariously at silly cracker jokes.

At last, when everyone had eaten as much as they wanted, it was announced that we had an important visitor, Father Christmas!

Amidst all the cheering and clapping that welcomed him, I always tried to guess who it was under the beard. Sometimes it was the voice that gave him away, and in the hearty tones asking if we had been good and telling us about his long journey from the North Pole, I identified Mr Fred Scott, the husband of the school caretaker, Mrs Scott. Nobody queried the fact that Santa had a Wiltshire accent! We were more interested in the sack of presents he carried. These were all carefully labelled, almost certainly by Mrs Perks, who must have been up half the night to get everything done. Our names were called out and we got up one by one to receive our presents. When this was over we all gave three cheers for the small army of parents who had provided the tea and helped with the games.

Parents quickly cleared away the remains of the party as paper plates had been used so that there was very little washing up. The infants were collected and the older children moved the desks back into their rows before standing behind them for a final prayer and lining up to go home.

On the last day of the Christmas term there were no lessons. There was a brief assembly before the Infants departed to their classroom. Those of us in the Junior class had a great deal of preparation to do. Firstly, we tidied our desks and handed in our exercise books. Paintings were removed from the walls and placed on our desks ready to take home. Two cupboards were tidied and our books placed on shelves ready for next term. One or two colourful posters were left up as well as the Christmas decorations as the Nativity Play would take place after lunch. Ink wells were given up to the care of two older girls who took them to the cloakroom for cleaning before slotting them back into the holes in our desks. Over the term pieces of soggy blotting paper had accumulated in them and needed removing before they could be made into pellets to be flicked around the room by naughty pupils. Then we had silent reading or designing Christmas cards out of scrap paper while Mrs Perks totted up marks.

There were not many prizes awarded this term because we had all received a present from Father Christmas the day before. We were allowed outside for a short break before returning to our desks and an unnatural silence descended as we waited to hear who had come top in their group for each subject. Mrs Perks announced the winners and small prizes of chocolate, crayons or books were awarded. I sometimes received a prize for composition (essay writing) as I was good at English. Eileen Parsloe was good at sewing and Christine Cuss was brilliant at several subjects including craft work. Wendy Barnes often won a prize for her interesting Speeches and Angela Gutteridge was very good at most subjects and she and Pauline Parfitt won prizes for their hard work. Several younger children were awarded prizes and praised for their achievements and progress. Sweets were handed round to everyone once or twice and we all felt suitably pleased with ourselves.

Mrs Perks had arranged an early lunch with Dora Spackman who delivered our lunches in metal cannisters, and this was consumed fairly speedily and the older children cleared plates and cutlery. Mrs Scott who washed the dinner things was busy transporting dishes to the small kitchen building for washing up. Desks were cleared to the sides of the room and chairs arranged in rows for the parents.

After a break we returned to the Infants' Room ready for the play. The room was chaos with chattering nervous children and several helpful parents assisting with costumes and applying stripy tea towel headdresses to the shepherds and crowns made from gold card adorned with coloured wine gum jewels to the three kings. Several tiny girls looked very sweet in white nightie gowns, tinsel head bands and angel wings. One would never have guessed that the most angelic-looking child had been in trouble only half an hour earlier for pinching a fellow pupil. At last the hubbub died down. Several small boys were frowned at for jostling each other and assumed innocent expressions as they were lined up in their queue.

The door to the Junior classroom was opened and we filed into our places, Juniors first to sit in rows behind the Infants. We all began with *Once in Royal David's*

City as the Christmas story was enacted once again with the Juniors narrating it as the Infants took centre stage and acted it out with the carols included as part of the narration. Then when the birth of Jesus had been announced and the doll placed in the crib, the Infants proudly sang *The Rocking Carol (We will 'wock' you!)* as I tried to bite back my giggles. Then the audience of parents beaming at their cherubic offspring, joined in the rest of the carols. After enthusiastic applause and thanks to parents and teachers it was time to go home. Several of us who lived nearby stayed behind to help tidy the room, and after wishing our friends and teachers a happy Christmas we departed to our homes.

SCHOOL PERFORMANCES

MY FIRST MEMORY of school performances was when I walked proudly down to the village school with my parents and brother M to watch my eldest brother, B aged ten, perform the starring role in the school production of *The Sorcerer's Apprentice.*

B was playing the part of the apprentice and much thought had gone into his costume. An old blackout curtain had been generously donated by the Reeves and this was easily converted into a cloak, after being turned up by our mother and gathered at the collar. It swirled beautifully as it was a large piece of material. Our father then became interested in B's part and cut out various chemical symbols and Greek alphabet letters such as

Omega. They were made out of stiff foil from the inner tops of coffee jars and other household items. These symbols and letters varied in size from two to three inches in height and were stapled to the cloak. B looked very impressively dressed and we all looked forward to watching his performance.

We sat in the school room expectantly as the makeshift curtain was drawn back to reveal the stage. B arose from his stool as the music rose in tempo and everyone gasped as his cloak swirled and glimmered in the light in a truly magnificent manner as he twirled about the stage. There were many approving comments on his costume and our parents were very pleased at the success of the performance.

I was really too shy to enjoy school performances, but the following year I had to play the part of a woodcutter and then come to the front of the stage to recite the story of *The Widow's Mite* from memory. At six years old, I was just realising that many words had more than one meaning. Previously, I had rather wondered if the mite had bitten the widow! Also, I was not the favoured person for the part. Mrs Perks would much rather have given the part to someone else, but my skill in reading and the fact that I had an excellent memory won me the part. I was rather cross that I did not have a pretty costume like some of the other girls. I just had dark grey trousers, an ancient jumper and my brothers' old wellingtons. However, Commander Jenkins, a school governor, very kindly came up afterwards to congratulate me on my performance, so I was very pleased.

We made puppets nearly every school year from the age of seven, as soon as we entered the Junior class, known as The Big Room. The faces of our puppets were first created by shaping a lump of plasticene into a head and neck, with a face on one side. The neck also had to be wide enough to fit one or two fingers to allow for greater flexibility in the puppet's head movements. Once this was done the head had to be cut vertically in two. Mrs Perks did this because a sharp knife was needed. The two parts of the head were placed on our desks flat side down and then the plasticene had to be rubbed with a thin layer of Vaseline before we began to make the puppet out of strips of newspaper glued on top of one another. After about six layers of newspaper strips had been glued on, the puppet was finished with a final layer of plain paper before being left to dry. then the Vaseline enabled us to pull out the plasticene without damaging our puppet heads. The two halves of the head were trimmed before being fixed together with a few more strips of plain paper glued over the join. Then came the fun part, painting the faces of our puppets. Since we liked to write puppet plays based on fairy tales, many of our puppets tended to be either witches or princesses and were painted accordingly. Wool was glued on the top and back of the puppet head to represent hair and scraps of material were stitched together to make an outfit, with the two arms made to fit our fingers. Accessories such as miniature broom sticks might also be made.

We were divided into groups of four or five and each

group had to plan and write a play using our puppets. Our classroom contained a tiny puppet theatre with curtains and we practised our stories using small props and with us reciting our stories as our fellow pupils acted out the parts with puppets. One I particularly remember was *The Princess and the Pea*, for which we used layers of felt for the mattresses and a small marble for the pea.

At the end of the Easter or Summer term, parents might be invited to watch our plays, although we first practised them in front of the infants who joined us in the Big Room for the occasion. Sometimes, Mrs Palmer, who lived in a tiny house adjoining the school, was also asked if she would like to watch the performance. One Summer, we acted out some plays in Mrs Palmer's front garden which was a tiny lawn whose gate opened onto the school playground.

MRS PALMER'S HOUSE

NEXT TO THE SCHOOL, in fact built against the end wall of it was a tiny house which the Reeve family told me was originally built for a school assistant back in Victorian times. This house only had two tiny rooms downstairs and upstairs. The windows had a wooden frame cut to make them resemble the much larger church style windows in the school building. There was a tiny garden with a picket fence and gate separating it from the school playground and the occupant had to go in and out via the playground.

When I was at the village school this house was lived in by an old lady called Mrs Palmer, whom I believe used to be a school assistant in her younger days. The house was unmodernised because I know that Mrs Palmer had the use of the modern school cloakrooms which had been added in the 1950s.

This house was pulled down in 1962, after Mrs Palmer died, but you could still see the patch of new tiling on the school roof where the cottage roof had joined on to it. The area where the house had been was tarmacked over and added to the school playground and it provided a space for some wooden sheds used to store games equipment.

Mrs Palmer's House (left), which joined onto the school; and the old Brewhouse (right), although beer was served from a shed on the corner (by kind permission of Arlene Bishop)

CHAPTER 19

THE OLD BREWHOUSE

ON LITTLE SOMERFORD CORNER beside the gates into St Anne's Cottages was the Old Brewhouse. People in the street could only see an old weathered door, grey with age and with a few remnants of cracked and peeling paint on it. There was a small hatch in the top part of it and below the hatch a ledge wide enough to hold a jug of beer and a couple of glasses. When we first came to Little Somerford it was still in use as a brewhouse. There was a small notice informing potential customers when the Brewhouse was open and occasionally, but not very often, we saw someone having a drink there, but after a few years it had closed.

Kate Reeve told me that the Brewhouse had been extensively used by the navvies who worked on the railway in the early nineteen hundreds. The Brewhouse beer would be cheaper than the beer served in the nearby public houses because the customers were outside and standing up (at least to begin with!). Kate Reeve informed me that when they were young there were often fights on the corner after some of the Brewhouse customers had had their fill of beer.

The old door was used as a village notice board as it was in such a central position and there were often notices advertising barn dances or a jumble sale. Eventually the Brewhouse was demolished and became just another fragment of village history.

CHAPTER 20

SWEETS

WE WERE NOT given sweets until we were three years old. Sweet rationing had only ended in 1954 and even though I was a tiny child then, I can remember my parents and brothers cheering the announcement on the radio news. From the age of three I was given an occasional square of chocolate by my parents, but never more than one square. We had sweets at Christmas, chocolate coins and sugar mice. Our parents sometimes had a box of Black Magic chocolates. These were really lovely and we were usually allowed one or two each. Chocolates in those days were satisfying in the same way that expensive chocolates are today. It may be the jaded palate of incipient old age, but some sweets do not seem to taste as pleasant as they used to, but my mother used to say the same thing! It may be that as one grows older ones taste changes. Most sweets in the 1950s and 60s were really delicious, particularly toffees.

When we were small, my brothers and I used to share a tube of Smarties once a week. The three of us used to stand at the low window seat in the living room at Fern Cottage, B would open the tube of Smarties and we first sorted them into colours, then B divided them according to the number of each colour. Odd ones were left until the end and we then chose our favourites from the remainder. Any squabbling over the final few Smarties would result in our mother eating them! We all liked the orange ones, but I also liked the red ones as I could lick them and then rub the Smartie on my lip to emulate my mother's lipstick.

From the age of five, we were given a very small sum of pocket money to spend on sweets in the village shop. This was probably to teach us about money. I only had two pence to begin with, but my brothers had a bit more because they were older! Two pence would buy chews such as fruit salad or liquorice chews which were a farthing each, four for one penny. The farthing was the smallest coin then. Sometimes I bought a banana split which was a flat piece of toffee about six inches long with a layer of banana flavoured chew in the middle. They were delicious and would last for ages.

After a year I progressed to three pence, the old thruppenny bit, pocket money. This was much better because it would buy me two ounces of loose sweets which were stored in large jars in the shop and made a wonderfully tempting display. I now had a much wider choice and spent ages in the shop deciding how to spend my wealth. Some of these sweets are not often available these days except in specialist sweet shops. There were round stripey peppermints known as bulls' eyes, liquorice comforts which were small strands of liquorice in a coloured sugar coating making them look like mini torpedoes. Dolly Mixtures, as their name suggests, were tiny sweets, some in stripey cubes, others like mini-jellies. Little girls liked them for dolls' tea parties. There were giant red or yellow pear drops which had a smell similar to nail varnish, mint imperials and winter mixture which was a mix of sweets such as clove drops and which all tasted like strong cough sweets. Aniseed balls were another favourite as although they had a strong flavour, they lasted for ages because they were too hard to bite. However, our mother did not like us eating them because they made our teeth look brown. There were chocolate cigarettes with edible paper which small children enjoyed because they could pretend to be grown up smokers, or white sugary imitation cigarettes with pink tips. There were also liquorice pipes with pink hundreds and thousands on the end to make the pipe look more realistic. Nowadays they would be frowned upon, but children enjoyed them. My brothers used to have a packet of chocolate cigarettes in their Christmas stocking.

Bubble gum was very popular then, but we were not allowed to buy it. It came in round chunks about three quarters of an inch across and half an inch thick and wrapped in paper. Occasionally we were given one by a friend. The lurid pink gum first had to be chewed to a soft consistency and then ones tongue could be gently pushed forwards into the gum mass and if one then blew gently, a bubble of gum flowed from ones mouth and subsided with a loud pop over the lower half of your face, whereupon it could be licked back into your mouth and the whole procedure repeated to the annoyance of parents who hated the habit. The gum soon lost its taste and soon after that the elasticity began to vanish so it could not be used to blow bubbles. Therefore when one became tired of chewing it, it had to be removed from ones mouth and put in a bin as it could not be swallowed. Thus began the problem of chewing gum on pavement or putty-like lumps lurking under school desks.

If I ever had sixpence to spend, which was a rare occurrence, I often bought a slab of Sharp's toffee which was really delicious and the pack came with a miniature metal hammer as it was very hard to break. Sherbet fountains and sherbet dips were also a favourite, especially in hot weather. The fountains consisted of a cardboard tube filled with sherbet with a liquorice straw in it to suck up the sherbet, but the sherbet dips were bags of sherbet with a toffee lollipop for dipping and licking; great fun.

We also enjoyed the tubes of sweets such as Rolos, Munchies, Spangles and Opal Fruits as well as Milky Way bars, Mars Bars and Bounties although I usually preferred to buy loose sweets because they lasted longer.

Gob stoppers which cost one penny each, really lived up to their name back then and would last for ages, especially as we frequently removed them from our mouths to admire the new layer of colour. There were also hard round lollipops called Swizzels which in appearance were a mixture of pink, orange and green swirly colours. They tasted like a fruity sherbet and had a powdery consistency. When I went to play with my friend Wendy, her mother sometimes gave us twisted sticks of barley sugar which could only be bought in Malmesbury and which we particularly enjoyed. However, one of my favourite sweets was a giant triangular mint humbug which were almost too big to fit in my mouth. They had a chewy toffee centre and were delicious, but almost certainly ruinous to our teeth. However, I am pleased to report that my teeth are still in working order despite my childhood sweet tooth.

CHAPTER 21

THE PIGEON LOFT

ON ONE OCCASION when I was about nine, M and I went to Street Farm to see our friend Nigel. Nigel was full of enthusiasm for his new hobby of pigeon racing and keen to tell us all about it. His father had bought him some racing pigeons as they already had a pigeon loft above their old wagon shed beside the farm gate. The loft had been built by the Reeve family when they had lived there.

Nigel explained that racing pigeons have to be carefully bred for speed and trained as young birds to practise flying back to their loft. They were trained by being released further away each time and rewarded with food and water in their loft. He had two pigeons entered into a race. They had had to be put into a wicker carrier basket and taken to the local Pigeon Racing Club. Then, after he had registered his bird and paid his fee for the race, along with all the other pigeons they would be transported to the race start some distance away before being released at the appointed time. One of them had already returned, but Nigel was waiting for the second pigeon to arrive. He clutched a notebook and pencil, ready to record its exact time. He was just telling us this when we saw the pigeon heading towards the loft and we ran to the wooden ladder at the back of the wagon shed and followed Nigel up it.

The ladder ended at a trap door and we eased ourselves through the gap and closed the door behind us. On one side of the loft was a row of nest boxes filled with straw. These were raised up off the floor of the loft. Several of them were occupied by bright-eyed pigeons cooing softly to each other and resting from their recent races. Not far away was a metal feeder dish standing on the floor. The dish had a central domed piece which was filled with corn which then flowed out of a circle of holes at the base of the dome into the circular saucer base. It looked like a miniature moat around a castle. There was also a water dish so that these pigeons had everything they needed to live a comfortable life. At the front of the loft was an open door which could be left open for returning pigeons to fly straight in or closed, to keep the pigeons safe. The newly-returned bird was already eating corn from the metal feeder and Nigel was able to catch it and carefully remove the band on its leg. He then released the pigeon and put the band into his timing clock which hung on the wall and recorded the time of the pigeon's return. We were able to take a close look at the pigeons. Each bird had an identity tag on one of its legs and they cooed softly when Nigel picked them up and gently stroked them. These were sleek, beautiful birds, far superior to the fat wood pigeons which came into our garden to eat the young vegetable leaves and who complained loudly: 'My foot hurts, Betty, my foot hurts!'

CHAPTER 22

TRIPS

BRISTOL ZOO

OUR PARENTS did not own a car and we did not have family holidays. Our parents told us that we were very lucky to live in a pretty village and that people who lived in cities visited villages like ours for their holidays, so until I was nine years old, I had never visited a zoo nor had a trip to the sea. However, at that time our Headteacher, Mrs Perks, decided that the Juniors ought to have a school trip to widen our horizons and asked who had visited a zoo or a beach in the past two years. Several hands were raised and Mrs Perks asked where they had gone. Several pupils had visited the seaside and two of them had been to a zoo.

Mrs Perks allowed our class to have a vote and since we all wanted to see wild animals a zoo trip was requested. At that time there were not so many programmes for schools on television. Our school did not have a television anyway, although we occasionally watched a programme at Mrs Perks's house and we did not have one at home and in any case television back then was black and white only as colour television had not been invented. It is hard for people to realise that now as we are so used to screens and films and television in colour, but if you wanted to see exotic animals, a trip to a zoo was essential.

Our parents had to make a small financial contribution towards the coach and mothers were invited to accompany their offspring. Many mothers in those days did not go out to work or did part time jobs as mothers were expected to look after infant children at home until they started school.

At last the great day arrived and we stepped into the coach at 8:30am in great excitement., clutching our packed lunches and bottles of squash. It was a forty mile journey to Bristol where the nearest zoo was situated and we whiled away the time by looking out of the coach window and discussing which animals we particularly wanted to see. My friend Wendy was keen to see the elephants, Christine wanted to see the monkeys and I wanted to see the big cats, especially the tigers. The air conditioning in coaches was not as good as it is today and Wendy began to feel travel sick.

'Don't be so silly,' said her mother, 'Of course you won't be travel sick. Have a barley sugar and talk to Ceri and count all the red cars you can see.'

At last we arrived and the coach pulled into the car park next to the zoo. We all filed off and our mothers made a mental note of our coach number and the time we had to return to it.

On this occasion my mother was on the trip, having taken a day off work for the occasion, and we walked round the zoo with Christine and her mother, Mrs Cuss. Our mothers enjoyed seeing the animals as much as we did. We followed the signs to the various enclosures and animal houses. I looked with awe at the variety and beauty of the animals and birds, although I felt rather sorry for the elephants and big cats because I did not think they could really enjoy a caged life. We spent some time admiring the monkeys and laughing at their antics as they leapt about their enclosure. We watched the sealions being fed fish by their keeper and marvelled at the penguins which walked in a lop-sided lurch, but were so agile in the water. It was wonderful to have the opportunity to see animals which I would never be able to see otherwise.

We had our picnic on a lawn and Christine and I finished our sandwiches quickly as we were anxious to see more animals, but our mothers were enjoying a sit down, a cup of tea from a thermos flask and a chat. We had to be patient. Suddenly, just across the grass we saw six children riding on an elephant which was being led by its keeper. We begged our mothers to allow us to have a ride too and hurried over clutching our sixpences. We were helped up onto a special multiple saddle on which six small children at one time were able to sit, three on each side. We had a metal loop to hold on to which we clutched as the elephant had to kneel in order for us to mount and we swayed as it rose up again before being led by the keeper on its walk. We swayed from side to side on our high perch in time with the movement of the elephant and I marvelled at the strength of this beautiful animal as we moved forwards along the path. Soon we turned round and headed towards the starting point before being helped down. Already there were more children waiting their turn for a ride, which made me worry about the elephant. Christine asked the names of the two elephants giving rides and was told that they were Christina and Wendy. We burst out laughing as our friend was Wendy. Thank goodness there was not one called Ceri, I thought, my brothers would have teased me endlessly.

We then hurried off to see the giraffes and zebras and smaller animals such as porcupines and snakes, which I did not really care for as I felt too close with only a glass barrier! Finally, we went back to see the tigers again. Bristol Zoo had a pair of white tigers which were very rare.

The hours passed very quickly and before long it was time to return home and we all piled onto the coach and found our seats. Mrs Perks counted everyone at least three times before deciding that we could start back. Children were chattering loudly about the animals as the coach driver negotiated the Bristol streets and drove out into open countryside again. Eventually we arrived back in our village and hurried home to tell our families about our day, only to relive our experiences the next day when we wrote essays about our trip. I never forget the white tigers and even mentioned them in my Eleven Plus essay on *The Tiger*.

COVENTRY CATHEDRAL

THERE WERE SEVERAL village outings of various kinds. The Women's Institute had days out for their members, usually venturing by coach further into the Cotswolds to places such as Bourton-on-the-Water where they could admire the scenery on the journey and have a garden visit and cream tea at their destination. On another occasion they arranged to visit the new Coventry Cathedral and my mother suggested that I accompany her.

My mother was always hectically busy on trip mornings, insisting on us washing and drying the breakfast dishes and making a last pot of tea. Only when we had ten minutes before the coach departed would my mother decide to change into smarter clothes and powder her nose. I was driven to extreme impatience at her attitude as we had to walk down to the village corner to catch the coach and I had seen neighbours walking down ten minutes ago and had informed my mother about this five times already.

At last I managed to persuade her to leave the house and we hurried down the road, me impatiently hurrying ahead, my mother stating that the coach would not go without us. At that point we saw the coach leave the corner and proceed up The Hill. I was very disappointed at the thought of missing our trip and sadly we turned back. Suddenly a car drew alongside and one of our neighbours, Mr Cecil Gawthropp, wound down his window and enquired if we had intended going on the trip.

'Well, we were going to go,' said my mother, 'but we've missed the coach now.'

'Jump in, quick,' replied Cecil kindly, 'we can catch them up, they won't have got very far.'

We leapt into the car and thanked him. Cecil turned the car at the Dauntsey turning and set off down the road and up The Hill after the coach. We soon saw it ahead of us and Cecil's car gained ground. At a safe place he overtook the coach and several WI members waved to us and pointed as we went by.

'We've caught them now,' laughed Cecil and pulling ahead a safe distance and checking that there was no other traffic he swung his car across the road to block the coach. The coach came to a standstill and Cecil waved to the driver, raised his hat and smiled as we hastily thanked him and scrambled out and climbed on board the coach to join the others. There were smiles and amused comments as we found our seats. Thankfully the coach driver was more amused than annoyed at Cecil's action. We were immensely grateful to him.

My mother had told me before our visit about the dreadful bombing of Coventry by the Luftwaffe in 1940 during the Second World War. At that time this was only twenty-two years previously so for all of us this was a very poignant visit. We walked around the new cathedral which had only recently been completed, admiring the beautiful stained glass windows and the memorials to the tragic night of the bombing such as the Cross of Nails. I was especially impressed by the beautiful statue of St Michael's Victory Over The Devil by Jacob Epstein which is mounted on the outside wall by the main door. Then we walked around the remains of the old cathedral which stands right beside the new one. A set of display boards told the story of the terrible bombing and charred roof timbers were on display to emphasise the destruction, yet the remains of this cathedral still held a gaunt beauty and majesty and each building seemed to emphasise and add to the beauty of the other. The bombed out remains of the old cathedral stood as a stark reminder of the horrors of war, the new cathedral represented hope for the future. This was the first cathedral I had visited and it made a great impact on me.

On the way home we stopped off at a public house which provided *Chicken in the basket* or *Scampi in the basket*. This was a very popular evening meal provided by public houses at that time. Chicken or scampi and a helping of chips were served in a small basket for a set price. We all enjoyed our meal and discussed our day. Most people had been impressed by the new cathedral and we returned home uplifted by our visit.

THE SUNDAY SCHOOL OUTING

FROM THE AGE of eight to eleven years I attended the village Sunday School which was held in the Church of St John the Baptist. Every summer there was a Sunday School outing which in those days was always to the coast. A trip to the seaside was a rare treat for us country children, living as we did in a county with no coastline. Weymouth, Bournemouth or Weston-super-Mare were the nearest coastal destinations and usually Weston-super-Mare was chosen because it was the nearest. There was no motorway near our area then, so the journey took a lot longer than it does today, usually nearly two hours each way, giving us about four hours at the beach.

The coach picked us up at Somerford Corner and picked up a few more people further down the village street. Mothers were laden with bags containing towels, swimsuits and packed lunches, while several children clutched plastic buckets and spades or blow-up plastic water rings. The journey seemed to take a long time as we were all impatient to get to our destination. A cheer went up as we saw the sea in the distance and our coach soon pulled into the car park. We quickly alighted and hurried down to the beach. The tide was half out leaving a wide inviting stretch of sand. Impatient children were helped into swimsuits and dashed to the shoreline to paddle. I did not have a swimming costume as there was no swimming pool near us and I could not swim yet, so I just tucked my summer skirt into my knickers so that I could have a paddle.

I helped some other children build a sandcastle and dig a small pathway to the sea so that the incoming tide could flood the tiny moat. My mother sat on a towel beside several other villagers and enjoyed the view and the sea air. The beach at Weston is slightly muddy in composition compared to some other places, but we loved it. I looked for tiny shells and interesting pebbles on the shoreline and took them back to show my mother.

Then it was time for our picnic. There was a pleasant sea breeze which made it impossible to eat a sandwich without getting sand in it, but we did not mind. I could taste the salt in the air on my lips and was glad to share the flask of tea which my mother had brought with us. After lunch we strolled along the promenade looking for an ice-cream to share and a stick of rock to take home for my brothers. It was then I spotted the donkey rides and begged my mother to let me have one. The donkeys were lovely, patiently allowing children to climb on their backs and quietly walking the same route they had already walked many times that day. They all had their names on their bridles and looked pleased with their life by the sea. I noticed that some of the donkeys were tied up nearby and had full hay nets and water; they were resting while the others were being ridden. I was pleased about this as there was a long queue for the rides and it indicated that the donkeys were well looked after.

We walked slowly back along the promenade breathing the sea air. The seaside smells of hot dogs and doughnuts mingled with the salty tang of the sea, so different from the country smells of Somerford. Then it was time to return to the coach and relax on the long journey home. We all slept well that night, tired out by the change of air and the sea breezes on our faces.

CHAPTER 23

REBELLION IN ASSEMBLY

THIS IS NOT strictly about the village, but is in keeping with Wiltshire Moonraker humour.

When I was in the Lower Sixth form at Malmesbury Grammar School there was a rebellion in Assembly. Behaviour in the school was very good. If so much as a sixpence went missing, the whole school was called into the Hall and the building searched until the lost item was found. The staff were very strict.

However, the boys in our year decided that they ought to rebel in some way. They could not do much or the headmaster would tell them to leave and do their A Levels elsewhere. They racked their brains trying to think of something subversive to do. At last they came up with a plan; they would not sing in Assembly. Every morning after registration the prefects led lines of pupils to the front hall and they filed in to take their allotted places. We had a hymn, prayers, a Bible reading and then notices, before filing out in silence and proceeding to our first lesson.

Normally the boys sang lustily so it was soon noticed that we were not making our usual loud noise. We were kept in at break time and instead of getting a cup of tea or coffee and chatting to our friends, we had to sit in the hall and sing hymns, overseen by duty staff.

Again, the boys did not sing in Assembly and once more we were all kept in at break and sang hymns in the hall. After the third lost break, the girls complained and after demonstrating that we could sing hymns satisfactorily, were let out. The boys however, continued to lose their breaks as punishment for refusing to sing. Eventually they became fed up with having no break time so they devised a cunning plan. They *would* sing in Assembly, but they would put on broad Wiltshire accents. Normally they spoke standard BBC English with no real accents at all.

The next day I spent the whole of Assembly laughing until I cried. The hymn was: We plough the fields and scatter/ the good seed on the land.

The boys sang at the tops of their voices: '*Weee plough the vields an' scatt-urrr the good zeeed on the lanndd ...*'

The staff could not object, the boys had been ordered to sing and sing loudly, in Assembly and that is what they did. For the rest of the term the hymns were sung in a broad Wiltshire accent. I have never enjoyed Assembly so much as I did that term.

Old Cousens, halfway up The Hill, Little Somerford

CHAPTER 24

HEDGES AND FOOTPATHS

WALKING DOWN Little Somerford Hill one late September afternoon when I was eleven, I stopped to chat to John Reeve, who, together with his brother Ernest, was cutting the hedges in Old Cousens, the field bordering the lower part of The Hill on the left hand side when going down. It was a very long hedge and I admired their work as they always did their hedging by hand, an immensely skilled job that was a joy to watch. Young saplings growing above the hedge were partially cut through the trunk with a bill hook and bent over and woven into the hedge to fill in any holes. The hedge was first cut on one side and halfway across on the top. Then the men came onto the road side of the hedge and cut that, first cutting aside any brambles or nettles at the base of the hedge before tackling the hedge itself. The cuttings were raked into small heaps as they moved along and later burned on a bonfire.

I asked how long it took them to cut the hedge in the whole field. John told me that they had cut half of the hedges the day before and he reckoned that they would finish that field later that afternoon. They each started in the same corner and worked away from each other, each having an approximately equal portion to cut. It also depended, I was informed, on whether they had a ditch to dig out. If there was a ditch on the field side then they would dig that out too to ensure good drainage and it would take longer to complete their work. If the ditch was on the road side of the field then the local council would have to dig it out, but the ditch on this field, although on the outside (road side) of the hedge, ran under a footpath level with the top of the field and John Reeve informed me that they had to make sure that the culvert carrying the drainage pipes under the footpath was not blocked by undergrowth from their hedge.

There were a number of footpaths and green lanes in the village and these had to be walked regularly in order to keep them open. Several times I was asked by Mrs Tyzack, who was on the Parish Council, which footpaths I had walked and if any had not been walked during the previous eight months, I was asked to walk them so that they could be kept open. There was a particularly lovely green lane at the top of East End Lane. Originally it had been the main road from Brinkworth to Little Somerford, but after Victorian times it had fallen into disuse. It followed the slope of the escarpment up to the main Malmesbury to Swindon road. There was a definite surface under my feet, it was not just a muddy track, but it was unmetalled and the surface was covered in moss and grass.

Until I was ten, East End Lane itself was unmetalled. The tarmac surface stopped just past the cottages at the bottom of the lane and the road thereafter was rutted by farm vehicles which meant that any walker had to pick their way carefully, especially in frosty weather when the ruts froze solid. It was quite awkward walking up the lane in the dark in such weather to deliver the evening newspaper to East End Farm right at the top. When I was ten, the lane was metalled all the way up and although walking up the lane was much easier I did feel that a link to the past had been lost.

CHAPTER 25

BEING NEIGHBOURLY

I WAS OFTEN sent to near neighbours as a child, to ask if they could spare half a loaf or a packet of tea. Usually they were helpful. On our side I often did good turns for neighbours. When Ernest Reeve had to be in hospital for tests, his sister, Kate, was upset because, coming from a very large family, she had never had had to sleep alone in the house and the prospect completely unnerved her. She asked my mother if she would sleep at Yew Tree for a night. My mother declined, but nominated me for the task.

I slept on, or rather in, the most wonderful feather mattress which I sank into and the mattress rose up around me like the softest duvet. It was an amazing experience and no bed since has ever lived up to it. I also went over on several occasions to wash Kate's feet for her when she was too old to be able to do this for herself.

I would be sent over regularly to Yew Tree to hang out or bring in washing when Kate was crippled with arthritis and needed crutches to walk. On sunny days I was dispatched to open bedroom or attic windows to air the rooms and later in the day to close them. If there was a bad thunderstorm I would go over afterwards to check that Kate was alright. On one occasion the high mansard roof of Yew Tree Farm was struck by lightning and I hurried up to the attic to check for damage. There was a strange smell in the attics, but luckily the roof was not damaged.

In icy weather I would go over to warn Kate not to venture outside as the cement area outside her back door was very slippery with frost. From the age of ten I would call every day after school at Kate's request and collect her letters for posting.

I was often called upon to help round up escaped animals. Often, they were cows from Street Farm, however, on one occasion it was a large sow which had escaped. My brother M and I rushed out into the road after being summoned by Nigel Maidment. John Reeve in Sunnyside, the cottage opposite, was at his gate wondering what all the fuss was about. On hearing that it was a large pig which was on the loose, John unexpectedly declared his intention of coming with us. John Reeve, M and I set off down the Dauntsey Road and a hundred yards down saw the pig, a huge pink Landrace sow, just ahead of us. As we closed in on it the animal turned with a dreadful snarl at M, and would have bitten him viciously on the arm. John Reeve had obviously anticipated this, being knowledgeable about pigs and he quickly raised the stout stick he used to help him walk and belted the pig soundly across the snout just as it was about to bite M. With a loud squeal the sow retreated and John Reeve hastily drew M back saying: 'Careful! They can give you a nasty bite, keep back a bit.'

Drawing us aside onto the grass verge, he used his staff to adroitly turn the pig back towards the village. We closed in behind it and followed it up the road. Soon, Jeffrey Maidment appeared, rattling a bucket of pig nuts and the sow readily followed him back to its farmyard. This is just one example of the way the older villagers kept a watchful eye over the children in the village and made sure that they did not come to harm.

One day when I was ten, our neighbour, Iris Gleed, happened to see me walking by her house and summoned me from the road. 'Ceri, I was hoping I'd see you go by. Could you go to the shop for me, I don't feel up to it just yet.'

'Of course I can.' I knew that Iris had very recently had her second daughter and I waited while she wrote a list for me to take to the shop.

I eagerly rushed down the road clutching the list and knowing that Mrs Huntley (Dot) in the shop would be keen to hear details such as the weight of the infant and her name, Jenny. In typical village fashion I returned not only with all the things on Iris's list, but a couple of variant things in case Iris might prefer that item, as well as a small, useful present from Dot and her very best wishes and delight at hearing such good news and the information that Iris could return anything which was not suitable next week when she was up and about. This was what being a villager was all about, interest in and care for your neighbours.

We often gave fruit to close neighbours where we knew it would be appreciated. We also frequently provided flowers and greenery for the church flowers when Dolly Iles needed help with this. When I organised the carol singing, I was always careful to inform elderly neighbours living alone that it would be us shuffling about in the dark outside their front window and not to be worried if they heard noises after dark.

In the late 1950s, there was a terrible influenza epidemic. We were all struck down with it, as were most of our neighbours, and after a few days we had hardly anything edible left in the house. One evening there was a loud knock on the door and investigation revealed a huge box of groceries which was wonderfully welcome as no one was in a fit state to crawl to the shop. We found out afterwards that all the families affected by the influenza plague had had one of those boxes. It contained all the groceries necessary to keep a family for about a fortnight and had been organised by our wonderful rector, Mr Lutley. We were very grateful and never forgot his kindness.

We were always aware as young children that villagers kept an eye on us; this was rarely intrusive, just a knowledge that we were watched over. It was never required, but we knew that we could knock on almost any door and request help if it was needed. This also reinforced good behaviour as we also knew that any transgressions would be reported to our parents within minutes.

*Cow and calf graze in the orchard next to Fern Cottage
and opposite Yew Tree Farm (B Vyner)*

CHAPTER 26

THE ORCHARD

THE ORCHARD, as we always called it, was the field immediately beyond our garden, lower down the Dauntsey Road. It was a productive orchard even in our time although all the trees have now gone. It originally was part of the parcel of land which went with Fern Cottage, as the stable which was partly in the garden of Fern Cottage and partly in the orchard attested. On official maps it is called Barn Ground because there were two barns in it. The orchard had been thoughtfully planted and there were a wide variety of apples, both for immediate eating and for keeping over the winter. A number of the apples were cider apples although these were good for cooking too. When the orchard was planted back in Victorian times, farmers might make their own cider.

The first apple to ripen was the beautiful Beauty of Bath, a smallish eating apple of rare flavour. It was an attractive apple to look at with a red and yellow streaked skin. We were often given a few because the apples would not keep for long. We also loved the red Tom Putt cider apples which had a tart but attractive taste.

We often helped to pick the apples which was quite a mammoth task each September as some of the trees were tall and large. We only picked the apples from low branches or picked up windfalls. William and John Reeve, who lived at Sunnyside at that time, would do the main work. They always worked together if ladders were needed as their eldest brother, James, had died after falling out of an apple tree in that orchard. That particular tree was always eyed with suspicion and considered to be '*a bad 'un,*' i.e. unlucky. I remember William and John Reeve discussing who should climb the ladder.

'I'll go up', declared William.

'No, no, let me go up,' replied John.

'No, I don't want you to get hurt,' stated William.

'Well, I'm goin' to hold the ladder and you be careful!' said John, holding the ladder firmly as his brother ascended.

I was allowed to help but instructed to handle the apples carefully so as not to bruise them. Picked apples were put into wicker bushel baskets – the size of large log baskets. First the apple had to be inspected; if it was bruised, as most windfalls were, it was put in the basket of apples for immediate use, otherwise it was placed gently in the other basket which was for keeping apples. These apples were stored on piles of straw in a shed, different varieties being stored in different areas. One such tree was an Egremont Russet. The russet apples had brown patches on their skin, but tasted beautifully crisp and sweet. They were eaters. Other apples that were grown included Ashmead's Kernel, Blenheim and Codling. I loved holding the apples in my hands, admiring the colour and pattern of streaks and blotches on their skin and breathing in their scent. Their smooth coldness always reminded me of putting my bare feet on the cold elm planks on my bedroom floor in the old cottage nearby.

The orchard also had a couple of pear trees and a plum tree, but the most beautiful tree was a grand walnut. Each year we helped to gather the walnuts. The green outer cases protecting the nuts exuded a yellowy-brown sap which stained our fingers and took several days to wash off. I remember Malcolm Stoneham, a neighbour's son, boasting at primary school that he was a heavy smoker.

'Yeah,' he remarked, 'seventy cigarettes a day I smoke!'

As evidence he pointed to the yellowy-brown stains on his fingers which had clearly been made by walnut stains. I laughed and was able to show similar stains on my fingers after we had both been helping to gather the walnuts in the orchard. We teased each other about this for several days until the stains wore off.

On the other side of the orchard there was a barn with one open side which fronted onto a small paddock. The paddock had a gate into the orchard. Inside the barn was a hayloft where barn owls nested and below that was an old wooden manger for hay. This manger was worn smooth with age. Sometimes our cats had kittens in it and if the owls were nesting there, the cats had to be moved into safer accommodation. Bullocks were sometimes over-wintered in this sheltered barn and fattened up until they were ready for market.

The small red brick barn on the edge of the field opposite Yew Tree Farm was not often used when I was a child. One day, when I was about nine I wandered across to look inside as the door was open and I had never seen inside that barn before.

'Oh, don't you come in 'ere!' stated David Gleed, who worked at Yew Tree Farm. 'This is where the old chap hanged himself. My old dad told me he hanged himself from that beam,' he said, pointing to it.

I stared at him aghast. I knew, because Kate Reeve had told us, that the previous tenant of Yew Tree Farm had hanged himself because he could not make the farm pay. There was not much water on the farm and apparently he spent all his time pumping buckets of water for his animals because he could not afford to sink a well. That was why, when the Reeves moved into Yew Tree, Mr Reeve immediately had a well dug and a water supply assured.

'I hate comin' in 'ere,' said David. 'I only use it to store straw bales so I don't have to come in very often.'

I glanced around at the barn and looked anxiously at the thick beam going across and shuddered. It was sad to think of the poor man driven to kill himself despite all his hard work. I hardly ever saw the barn door open again.

AT THE END of the orchard was the railway line on a high embankment which made the orchard a sheltered place for wildlife. In the far corner of the field, next to the Dauntsey Road was a pond which was an old clay pit. We never played near that because it was deep and anyone who fell in would struggle to get out because your feet would stick in the clay at the bottom.

Many birds visited the orchard. Little owls and lesser spotted woodpeckers nested there. Thrushes and nightingales sang in the walnut tree and blackbirds and starlings hunted for worms beneath the trees.

On one occasion, our grey and white rabbit, Yogi, decided that he did not want to return to his hutch after his free run around the lawn and he squeezed through a tiny gap in the hawthorn hedge into the orchard. This was very worrying as there were wild rabbits at the bottom of the orchard and if Yogi joined them, we would never get him back. I rushed right round the house to the small area of fence where I could climb over into the orchard. As I was about to approach Yogi, I saw a cow taking an interest in the rabbit as it crouched in the grass. Yogi froze as the cow hastened over to him and whether the cow mistook the rabbit for a small calf, I do not know, but it proceeded to lick the rabbit over its back and nudge it with its nose, as it would a calf. Yogi appeared terrified, but luckily he did not move and after a few minutes the cow moved away after getting no response. As soon as the cow was at a safe distance I darted forwards and grabbed the shocked rabbit and carried him back to his hutch, telling him it served him right for running away.

IN SPRING IT was always wonderful to see the joyous exuberance of cows released from their winter shed and free once more to graze the sweet grass. The normally calm and contented cows rushed around in great excitement, kicking their back legs in the air, their tails askew as they stretched their legs and smelled the fresh air. They were clearly delighted to be let out and knew that this heralded long summer days grazing the lush grass.

The field is still there, but the old barn where the owls nested has been demolished. The other old barn still stands by the roadside, though almost destroyed by invasive ivy. Its old wooden door has long-since rotted and it is now a ruin. Until 2023 the walnut kept a lonely watch, but to my great sadness I heard recently that that was felled too. I hope very much that in the future the orchard will be replanted, that the owls and woodpeckers might return and that one day small children will be picking up windfalls and learning about the old apple varieties.

View down the orchard today
(by kind permission of Arlene Bishop)

CHAPTER 27

CHANGES

VILLAGERS WERE well provided for during the 1950s in that it was normal for food shops to provide deliveries to the surrounding locality. Quite apart from the daily post and milk, Adyes the grocer in Malmesbury had a green delivery van which came round twice a week with a small stock of general supplies and villagers could request an item to be brought for them the next time the van came around.

By the 1960s however, this had stopped as villagers preferred to get the bus into Malmesbury and have a wider choice of foodstuffs. Although fewer people had cars, buses to Malmesbury and back were hourly then. A butcher also came round the village several times a week and meat could be ordered, but again by the 1960s this had stopped. This had been a delivery by Caudell's the butchers who had a shop in Great Somerford, but their shop in Great Somerford closed and their shop in Malmesbury did not do deliveries to our village.

There were daily deliveries of milk and back then milk was always stored in clear glass bottles with a foil cap. Some bottles had the name of the dairy in relief on the outside of the bottle, however the Corn Gastons Dairy in Malmesbury had its name in bright scarlet and this made the bottles especially attractive. Different coloured foil tops specified the milk in the bottle, for example full fat milk (silver foil), semi-skimmed (green foil), or extra creamy (red foil). At school, children were issued with a small third of a pint in their morning break and this had to be consumed before we were allowed out to play. School Milk was a government initiative which had been established in 1945 to combat childhood malnutrition. I'm sure it did us good, except perhaps those poor children who were allergic to cows' milk. We enjoyed the milk best in snowy weather when the milk froze and expanded enough to rise about an inch above the bottle, with the foil cap perched on top at an angle like a schoolboy's cap. We enjoyed this frozen delicacy, but sometimes it was pecked at by blue tits and a small part of it had to be discarded. The milk bottles were recycled every day as the milkman took away the empties. The foil tops were collected too, sometimes for charities if they appealed for them and sometimes for school craftwork. Keen gardeners would put the foil caps on a string and hang them across their vegetable seedlings to deter pigeons. Householders would put out their empty milk bottles on their doorsteps and the milkman would collect them as he delivered the day's milk early next morning. A note in a milk bottle would request extra milk as required or cancel the delivery for a few days if people were away.

A drinks lorry also came round the village delivering crates of whisky and beer. The lorry also delivered soft carbonated drinks such as Tizer or Corona, this last not to be confused with the beer of that name. These carbonated drinks had a rubber stopper attached through the neck of the bottle with strong wire so that the stopper could be replaced after a drink was poured in order to keep the remaining drink fresh and preserve the fizziness. We were never allowed to have these fizzy drinks as, apart from not being able to afford them, our parents told us that they were bad for our teeth. We collected empty bottles from neighbours and returned them to the village shop as there was a refund of one penny per bottle, and we sometimes earned a few pennies that way. The refund also meant that there were no discarded bottles around the village and nearly all bottles were recycled. There was hardly any litter around the village ever.

Mr Bob Greenway, who lived at Lea between Little Somerford and Malmesbury, ran a bread delivery round and came to our village twice a week with a van load of bread, cakes and biscuits. Mr Greenway was extremely kind and often let us have bread on account as our parents were out when he came round. If we happened to be out, he would open the front door which was never locked during the day, and place a couple of loaves on the small shelf by the front door. The bread delivery continued throughout our schooldays until Mr Greenway retired in the early 1980s.

There was a van which delivered paraffin and lamp oil during the 1950s. This came round once a week, but we usually obtained our paraffin from the village garage.

Newspapers were dropped off at the garage and sorted

and delivered by a village boy, a local lad of thirteen or so. There were daily papers and the much read Wiltshire Gazette & Herald which is a weekly paper. Both my brothers did paper rounds when they were teenagers, which meant that if they were ill or the weather was bad, I had to help too.

There was also a Rag and Bone man who came around in a small pony trap during the 1950s, calling out for any discarded items. I always liked to look at the pony and occasionally would be sent out by my mother to ask if he would take away some item of rubbish. He did not pay for small items of scrap. However, he was the last of his kind. By the time I was eight, the Rag and Bone man was consigned to history.

THROUGHOUT OUR SCHOOLDAYS we heard the clang of milk churns twice a day. Milk churns were put out on a special stand near the farm gates. At Yew Tree Farm there was a wooden stand at the end of the drive, but at Street Farm the churns were put out on the old mounting block. After the morning milking eight or ten churns full of milk would be put out and then a short time later at about eight-thirty they were collected by lorry. The driver would unload empty churns ready for the afternoon milking and return to the dairy. He returned at about half past five in the afternoon to collect the village milk and put out empty churns for the morning. There were only about twenty-two cows at Yew Tree Farm and about twenty-six at Street Farm. During the early nineteen seventies, the milk was collected by small tankers, but then it was decreed that the farms had to supply a whole tanker load of milk to justify the expense of collection, and so began the decline of the small farms and the beautiful sight of contented cows grazing small meadows became a rarity. Many village farms were small and farmers did not always have the facilities such as enough grazing, or fodder, or barns large enough to provide a larger herd with shelter during the winter. I missed seeing the cows and I know that several local farmers were devastated when they had to give up keeping them.

The main drainage was put through the village in the early 1960s and many villagers were pleased to have bathrooms and indoor flushing lavatories rather than tin baths and outside privies. Our house was never connected so we had to endure the original primitive conditions. When the drainage trench was dug, there was a layer of quartz about eighteen inches down from the surface and if we peered in the trench in our road on our way home from school, the workmen would tease us by saying, 'Want some diamonds?' and they would hand us a chunk of large clear quartz crystals which we loved because we had never seen anything like them before. Being one of the older children at the village school then, I was amused to hear several small boys boasting about their 'diamonds' over the next few days.

Whenever the road near our house was resurfaced, I always watched the large steam rollers with their huge, heavy wheels, moving slowly backwards and forwards as they compacted the new tarmac. The old steam rollers were fascinating to watch and I think that they were more interesting than the modern vehicles today.

Hardly anyone locked their doors during daylight, unless they were going out for the whole day and even then, several villagers said to me: 'Just in case anyone needs to get in when I'm not there, I keep my key under the white stone by the door/ under the basket in the shed/ on the beam over the porch.'

THERE WAS AN old Victorian Post Office building next to the garage which had been used until the Second World War. It still had the old sign up for many years. When we first moved to Little Somerford, the post office was run by Mrs Polly Atkinson who ran it from her small cottage on the village corner. It was one of two cottages named St Anne's Cottages then. Mrs Atkinson's house was on the right when you faced the cottages. I remember going in there every week with my paternal grandmother when she went to collect her pension. Granny lived with us for a couple of years after we moved to Little Somerford. I was only about two years old then and Granny would lift me up onto the counter so that I could see what was going on. After collecting her pension, Granny would usually buy a quarter of a pound of chocolate covered caramels and if I was very well behaved she would give me one. Mrs Atkinson had just two or three jars of sweets behind the counter, she was not competing with the village shop. After a few years, Mrs Atkinson died and the service was taken over by Mr Brian and Mrs Pamela Tyzack who ran the post office from their house, Mills Farm, opposite the garage. Our post was first delivered by Mr Mike Young who lived in Great Somerford, but he emigrated to Australia in the early 1960s and Mr Tyzack took over the postal deliveries. There was a post box on Somerford Corner, but occasionally it was out of use as small birds regarded it as a safe nesting box.

The village had its own red telephone box in the 1960s and all phone calls from the box went to the exchange via the post office. The post office staff were always very well informed. The telephone box stood near the garage on The Street. Many houses did not have a telephone at that time and the phone box was well used for a number of years.

The biggest change in the village came in 1963 when the Vale Leaze housing estate was built. I had mixed feelings about this as it was built on Butcher's Orchard, a field where wild bluebells and dog roses grew in the hedgerows and patches of cowslips adorned the upper slopes in spring. The new houses were unattractive in my view and did not blend into the landscape as the old cottages did. On the other hand, the people who came to live there were very pleasant. They brought new life to the village school and Women's Institute and were undoubtedly a good thing for the village.

And so we come to the end, but only of my reminiscences. The village continues to exist, to change, to evolve. Little Somerford is still there, creating current memories for its inhabitants to add to those of mine of the 1950s, 60s and 70s.

The layers of history continue to build on this small, but much loved, Wiltshire village.

ACKNOWLEDGEMENTS

I would like to express my sincere thanks to Lorna Brookes of Crumps Barn Studio for all her help with the production of this book and for encouraging me to write more about our life in Little Somerford during the 1950s and 1960s.

I am immensely grateful to Francis Chamberlain who read most of these pieces as soon as they were written and who made suggestions about further topics.

Thanks also to Andrew Walkland for reading the manuscript and saying that he enjoyed it!

Special thanks to the following friends in Little Somerford and Cleverton: Richard and Lin Boulton for letting me relate a memory of Mrs Dolly Iles. Robert and Julie Gawthropp for allowing me to include a memory of Cecil Gawthropp. Caroline and Oliver Jones Davies for permitting me to include the piece on Yew Tree Farm, together with the photo. Especial thanks to Caroline for giving me a wonderful grand tour of the farmhouse as it is today. Nigel Maidment for allowing me to include the pieces on The Gateway and The Pigeon Loft. Martyn and Pauline Scott who let me mention Mr Fred Scott and Mrs Eileen Scott. Malcolm and Christopher Stoneham for letting me include the memory of Mr Ken Stoneham and the 'Walnut' memory.

I am indebted to my friends: Wendy Garside, Pauline Jones, Angela Smith, Christine Sparrow and Eileen Webb who all attended Little Somerford School with me and did not object to being mentioned in this memoir.

Grateful thanks to the following friends who allowed me to use their photos: Arlene Bishop for providing several photos of the village school and the old brewhouse. Thank you, Arlene, also for constant encouragement in my writing. Hector Cole for giving me permission to walk over his fields to take photos of the dewponds. Also for identifying the different parts of the old farm buildings in Old Cousens. Mr Trevor House, for having a rare photo of the hollow tree in the field behind the Old Rectory. Nigel King for providing a photo of Little Somerford Garage, taken by his uncle Mr Geoffrey Snelgrove.

I am very grateful to John, Kate and Ernest Reeve who throughout my childhood, talked to me about their farm and the village, showed me the old farming tools in The Hut and allowed me to help gather apples and walnuts in the orchard.

Finally much love and thanks to my husband, John for reading my book and listening to endless tales of Little Somerford.

ABOUT THE AUTHOR

CERI VYNER was brought up in North Wiltshire. Her career has included teaching and bookselling. Ceri is married and lives in Norfolk. Her hobbies include reading, history, enjoying museums and galleries, visiting Italy and collecting Delft tiles.

She is the author of two personal histories about life in 1950s Little Somerford, *Let'n Went!* and *'Ow Bist*.

'Ghost stories, tales of the railway, village scandal –
it is all here and deftly woven together'

Let'n Went!

The delightfully personal story of life in 1950s
Little Somerford, North Wiltshire

ISBN 9781915067142

OUT NOW